VINTAGE HOMES

ADULT COLORING BOOK #2

ANTIQUE VICTORIAN HOUSE DESIGNS IN QUEEN ANNE & OTHER CLASSIC STYLES

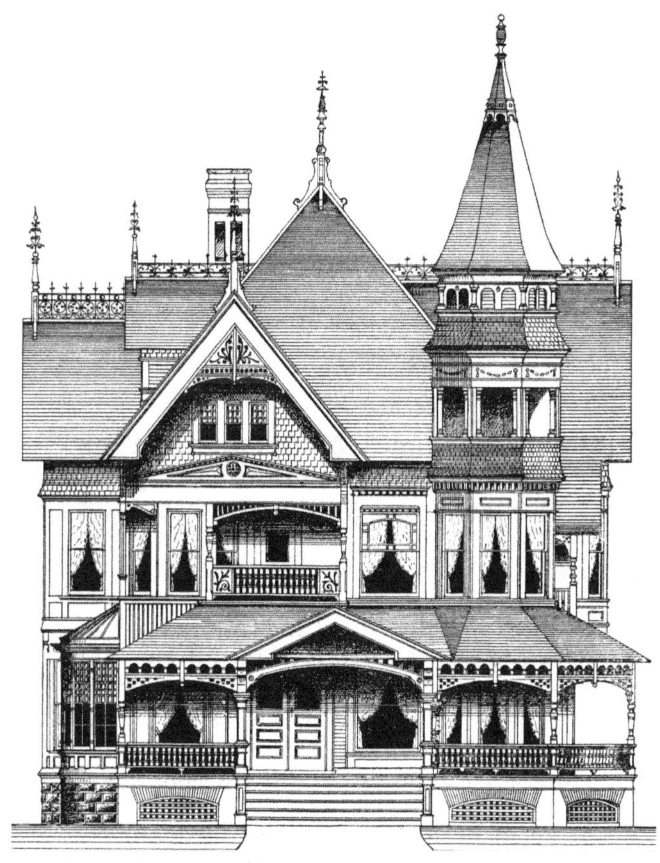

FROM THE EDITORS OF CLICK AMERICANA®
CLICKAMERICANA.COM

INTRODUCTION BY NANCY J. PRICE
EDITOR-IN-CHIEF, MYRIA.COM & AUTHOR OF "DREAM OF TIME"

A few other books you might enjoy...

Vintage Homes: Adult Coloring Book: Luxurious Victorian Houses & Mansions

Vintage Women Adult Coloring Books series, featuring fashions from the past

The Beer Lover's Guide to Vintage Advertising

Something Old: Vintage Wedding Dress Fashion Look Book

Dream of Time, by Nancy J. Price (a time travel novel set in San Francisco, 1900)

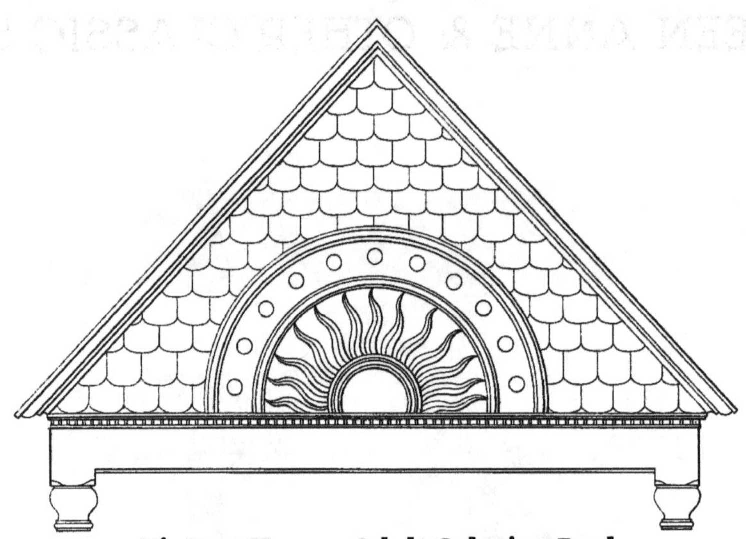

Vintage Homes: Adult Coloring Book
Antique Victorian House Designs
in Queen Anne & Other Classic Styles

Published by Synchronista LLC – Gilbert, Arizona, USA

www.Synchronista.com

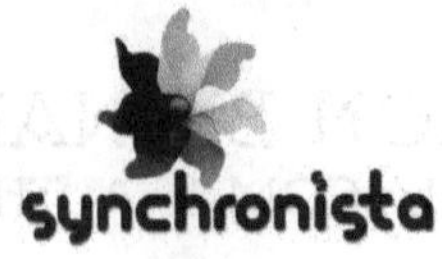

INTRODUCTION

The most charming homes of the later Victorian era were a sight to behold, from their complex structures to their ornate crafted details.

Inside this book, you can take a look back to the 1880s and 1890s, when many elaborately-decorated houses were built in America.

These 44 authentic antique home designs have all been drawn in the architectural elevation view — as if seen straight-on from the front. Many of these houses include wonderful wide porches and balconies, cupolas, turrets and towers, steep roofs, shingles, and ornate moldings and trim.

Broadly, the homes in this book are in the Queen Anne style, with many in the Stick or Eastlake style, though some may be considered Folk Victorian, with "gingerbread house" (bargeboard/vergeboard) detailing. Most of these houses were built from wood, with many different textures, patterns, carvings and other ornamentation incorporated into the design. (In many ways, the decorative elements would be the style's downfall, since the exterior wooden adornments that eventually broke off or wore away were costly to replace.)

But what about the color? In addition to the creative, crafty styles of architecture, advances in manufacturing made a rainbow of paint shades affordable, and the homes that remain from this time are often vividly colored.

While fans of Victorian architecture will likely admire each stunning image, these elaborate illustrations will be of special interest to experienced colorists thanks to the beautifully-detailed originals.

The homes from this age that remain standing today are considered historic treasures — which is all

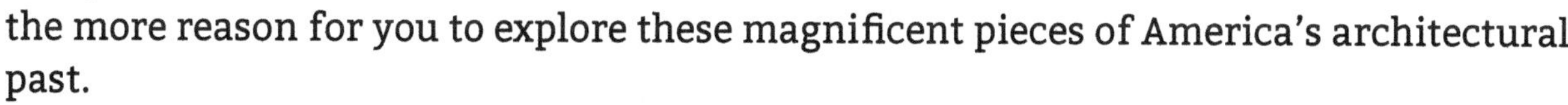

the more reason for you to explore these magnificent pieces of America's architectural past.

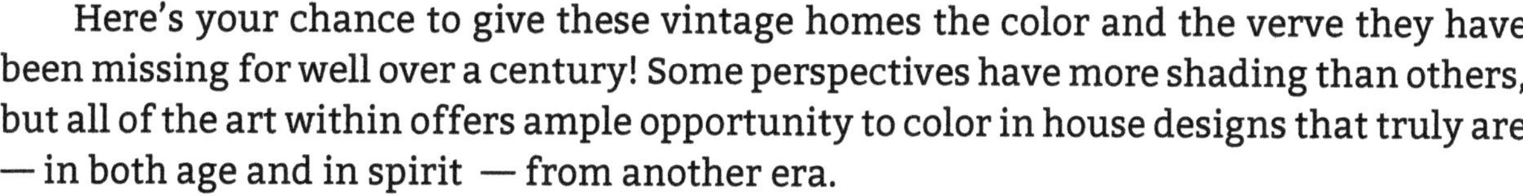

Here's your chance to give these vintage homes the color and the verve they have been missing for well over a century! Some perspectives have more shading than others, but all of the art within offers ample opportunity to color in house designs that truly are — in both age and in spirit — from another era.

Best,

Nancy J. Price
Founder, Click Americana
Editor-in-Chief, Myria.com

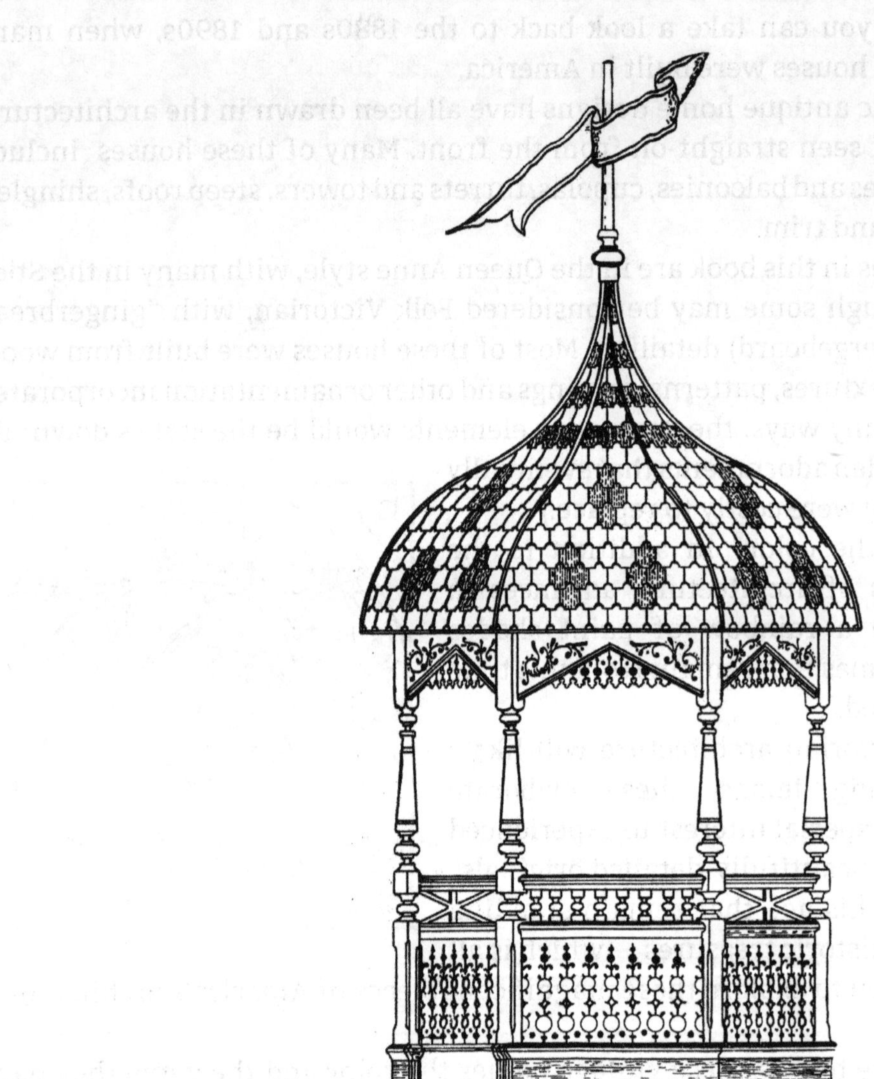

Important Notes

Within these covers, dozens of authentic home illustrations have been rediscovered and transformed into coloring pages. Every one of the antique images in this book was carefully chosen, then painstakingly restored by hand using modern technology in order to return it to its original glory as much as possible.

Before creating this collection, we reached out to coloring book fans, and incorporated as many of their suggestions as we could:

- Each highly-detailed antique picture is printed only on one side of the paper, allowing you to color with your choice of medium without worrying about bleed-through to an image on the back.
- While many people have reported excellent results using colored pencils on designs like these, if you use pens or markers, you may want to slip a blank sheet of paper (one at the end of the book) behind the page as you color to avoid bleed-through. Pages 6 & 7 offer space to test your coloring medium of choice.
- Page numbering, titles and other image information appears on the reverse of each page, ensuring the coloring side is distraction-free and could be suitable for framing. The coloring pages themselves do not have page numbers visible on the front. To navigate using the index, found on the following two pages, please reference the numbers opposite each picture.
- We have included all floor plans provided, however, not every level is depicted.

Although these pictures were not created with colored pens, pencils, crayons or paints in mind, we reviewed hundreds of drawings to select those most suited to the task. Still, due to the authentic vintage nature of the artwork, this isn't a typical adult coloring book of modern images with pristine lines.

The images were restored as faithfully as possible, but since the original artwork is not known to exist, we relied upon high-resolution scans of the printed newspaper pages. As such, there are a few caveats:

- Borders, shapes and lines are occasionally incomplete.
- Some details have been lost due to printing processes and quality of preserved books.

In addition, in keeping with the original designs, you will also see...

- The pictures are often very intricate.
- There are large areas of black on certain pages, and considerable amounts of shading included in many of the images.
- There's a sketch-like quality on some illustrations, particularly near the edges.
- We chose not to over-simplify the artwork because of the tremendous amount of detail (and personality) that would be lost in the process.

We hope these hand-drawn snapshots of history in the making inspire your muse — and we would love to see how you bring color to these beautiful Victorian homes! You're invited to post your creations on the book's Amazon.com page. Thank you!

VINTAGE HOME DESIGNS COLORING BOOK PAGE INDEX

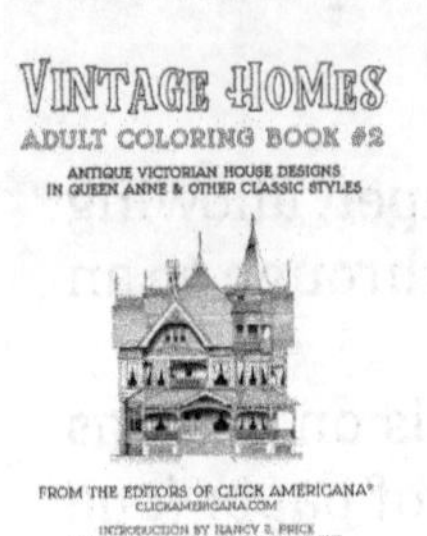

↑ Page 1

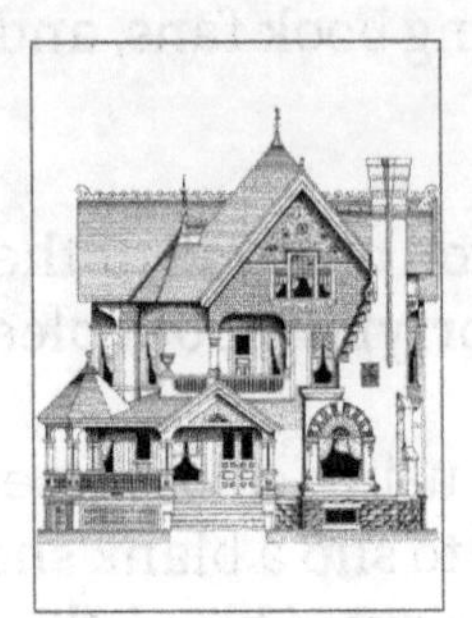
↑ Page 13

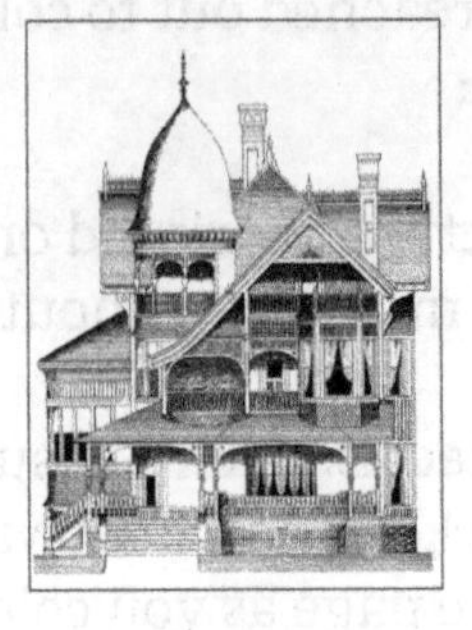
↑ Page 15

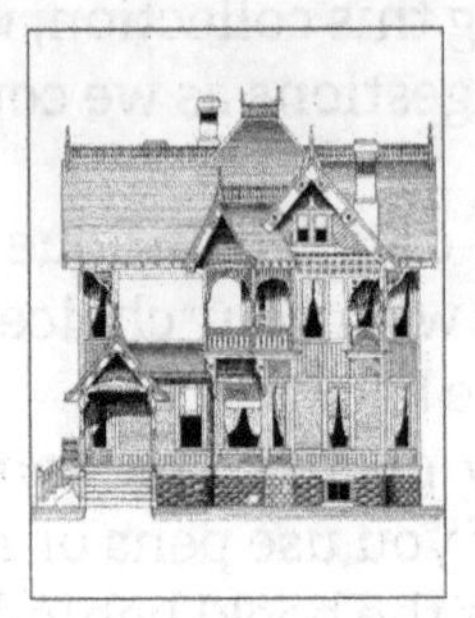
↑ Page 17

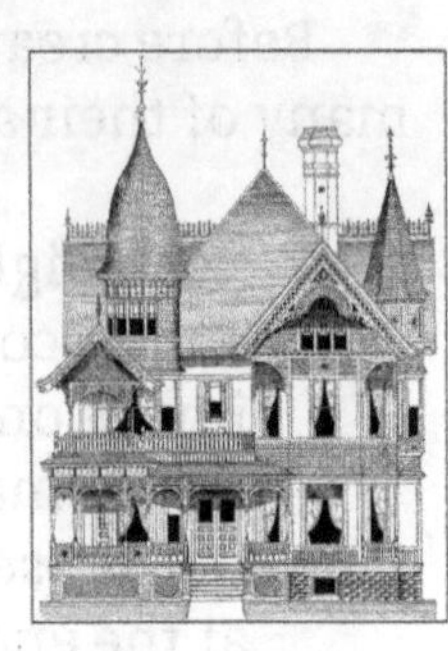
↑ Page 19

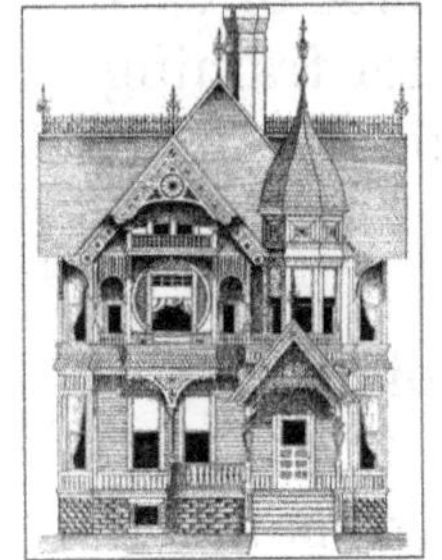
↑ Page 21

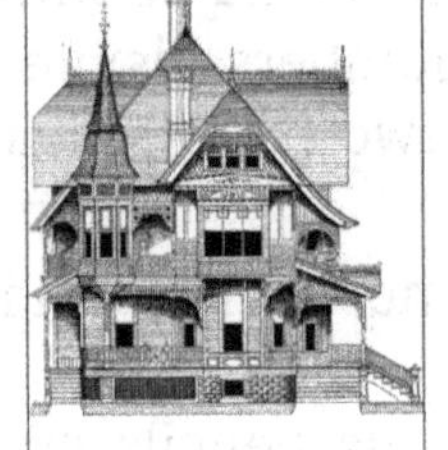
↑ Page 23

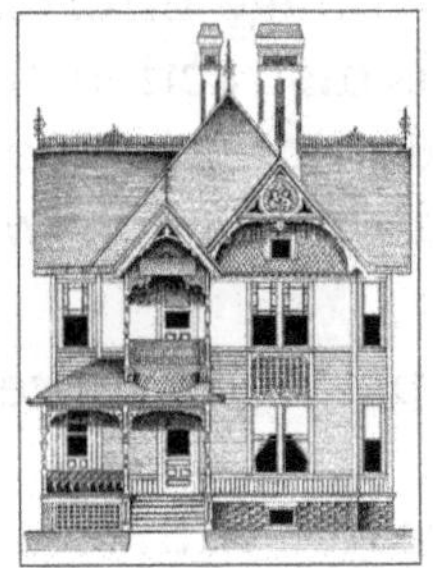
↑ Page 25

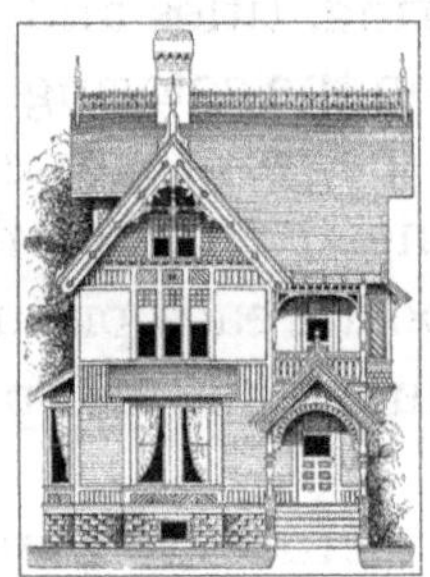
↑ Page 27

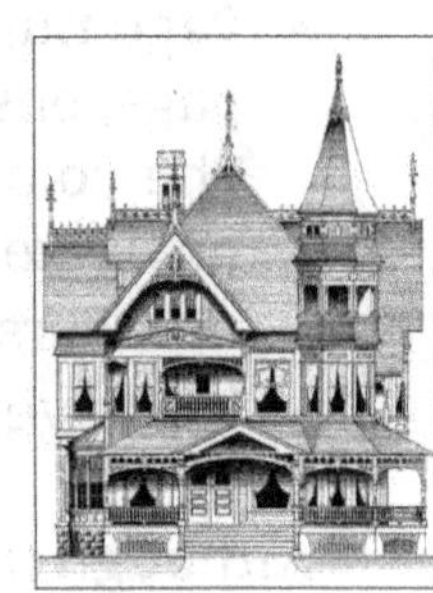
↑ Page 29

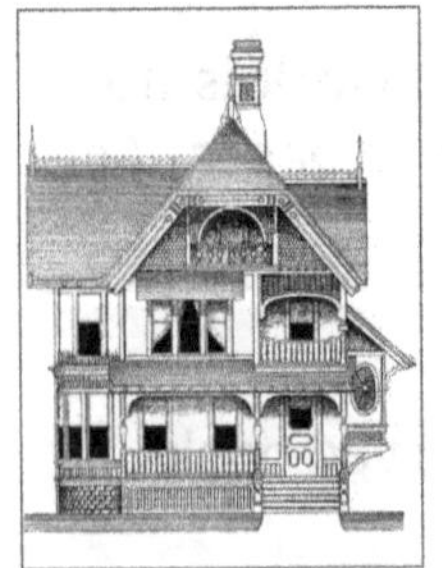
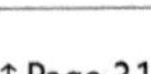
↑ Page 31

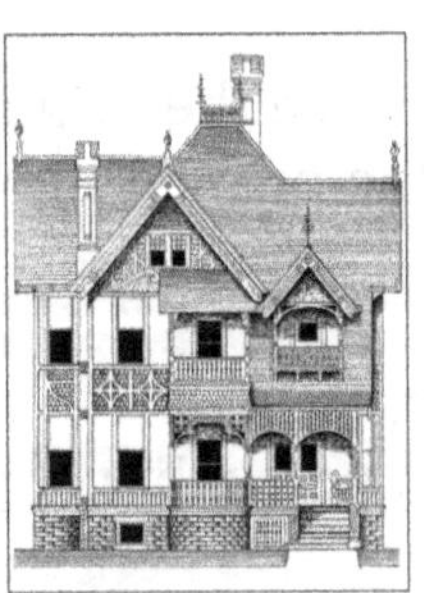
↑ Page 33

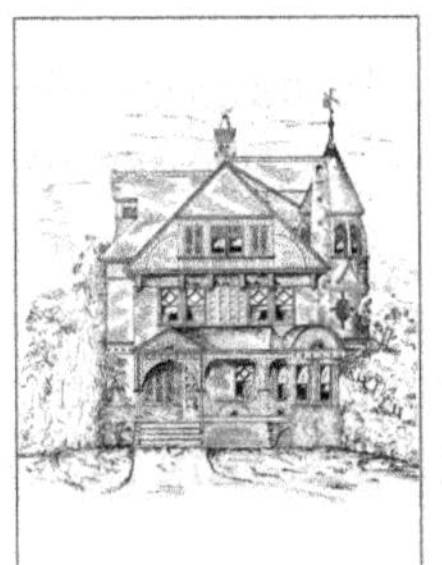
↑ Page 35

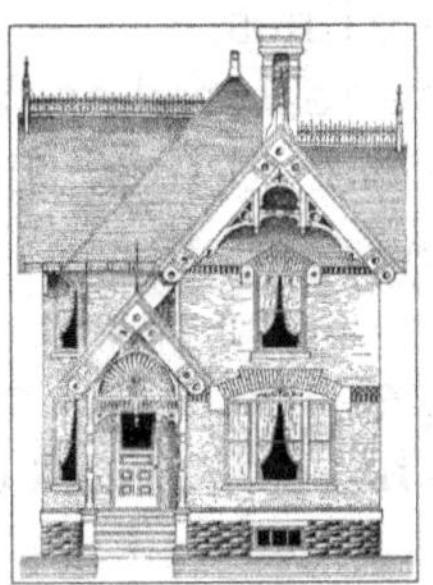
↑ Page 37

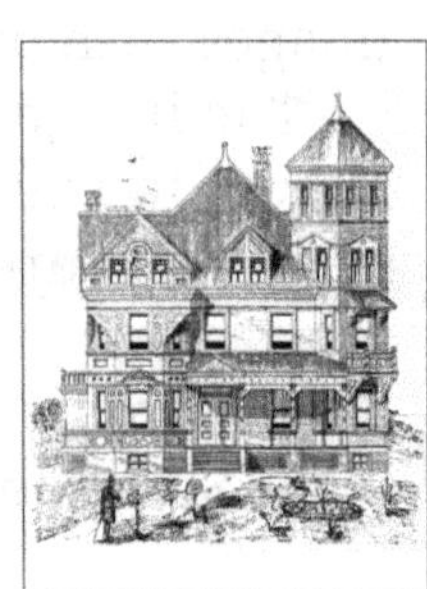
↑ Page 39

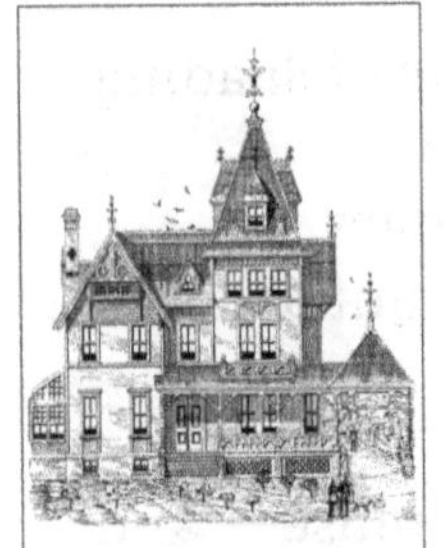
↑ Page 41

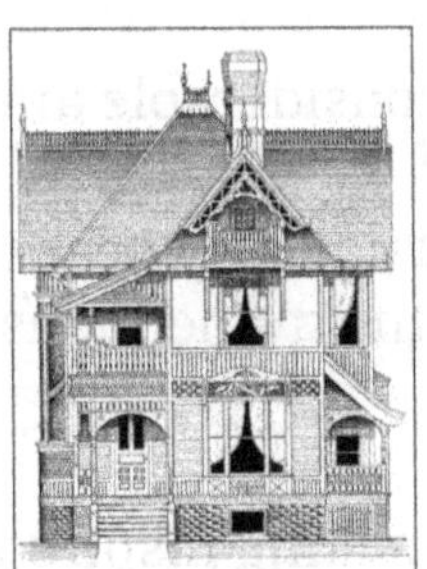
↑ Page 43

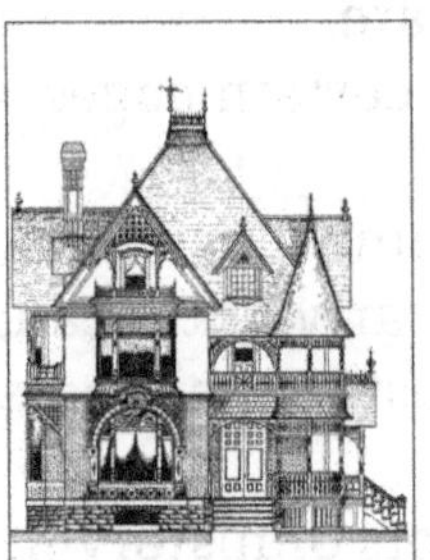
↑ Page 45

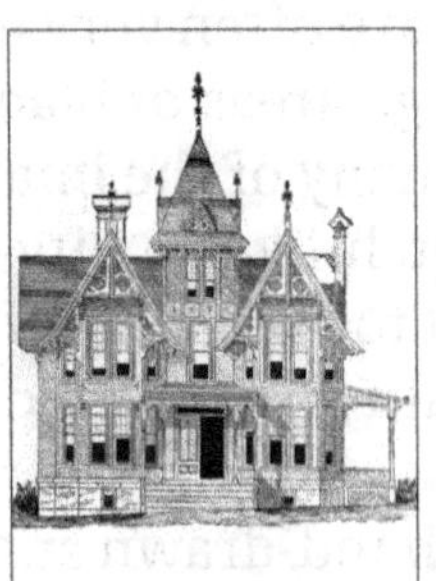
↑ Page 47

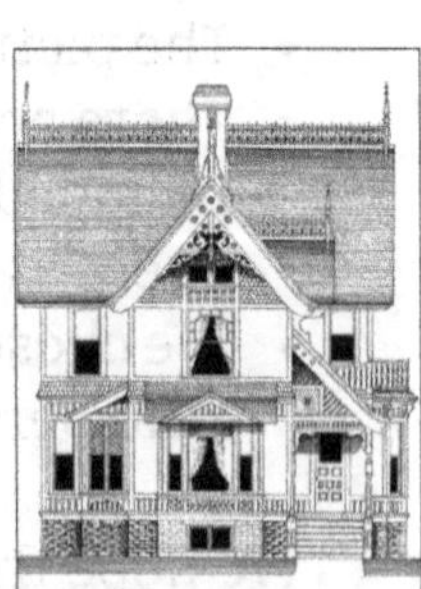
↑ Page 49

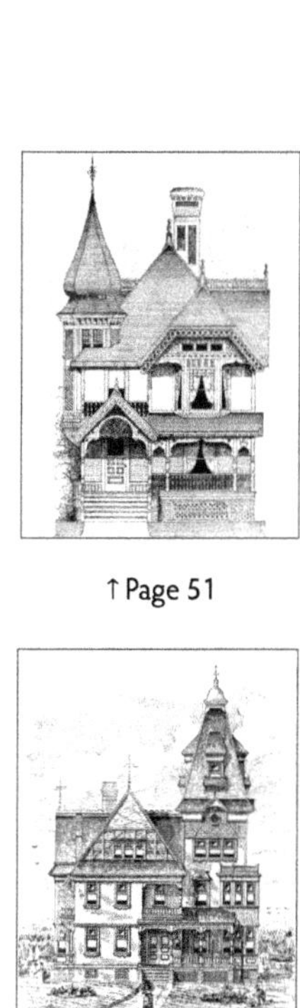

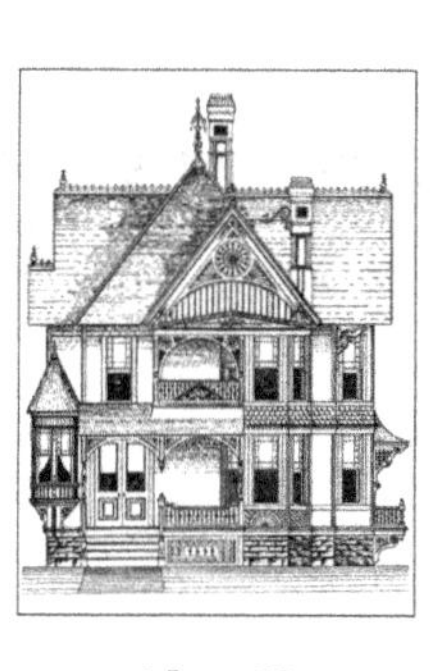

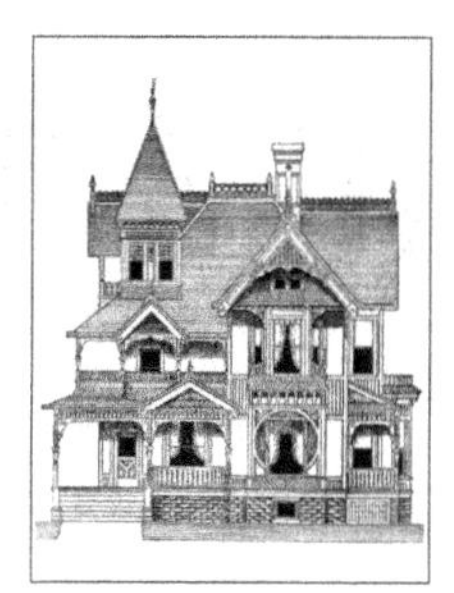

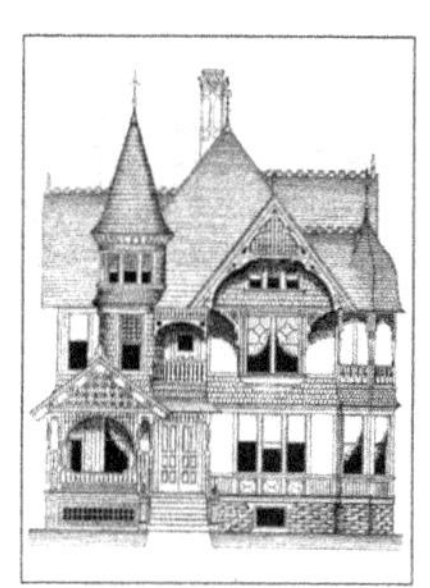

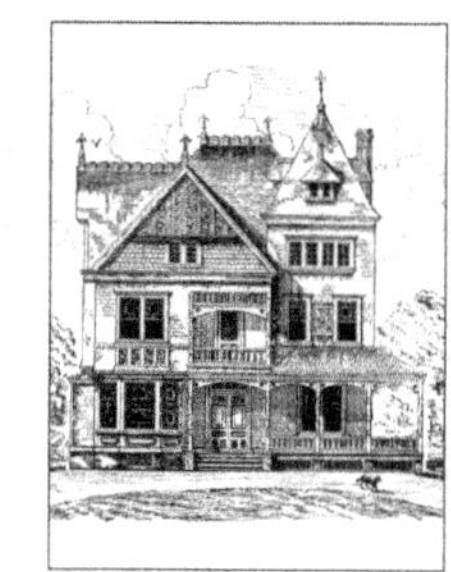

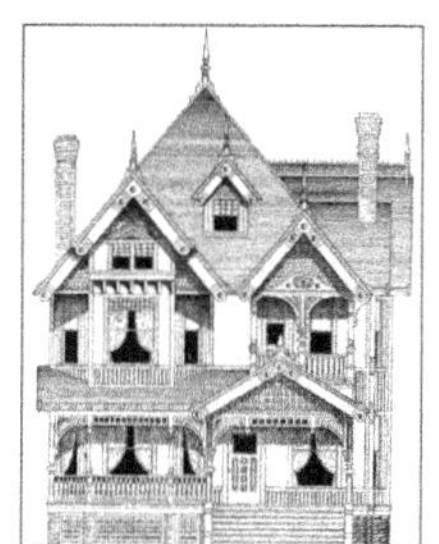

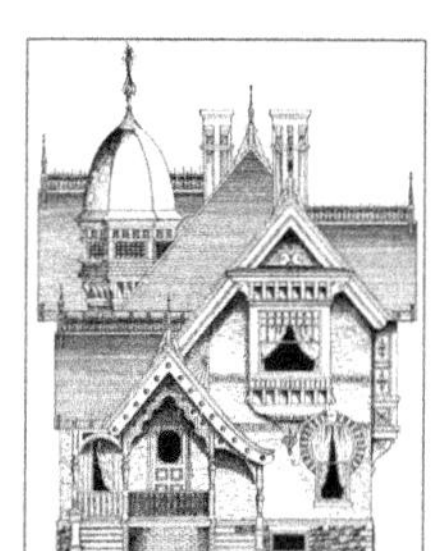

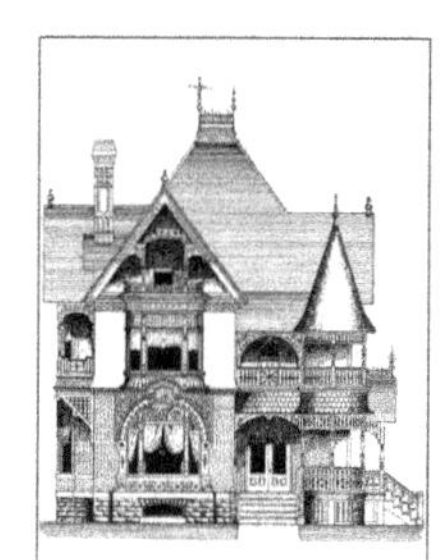

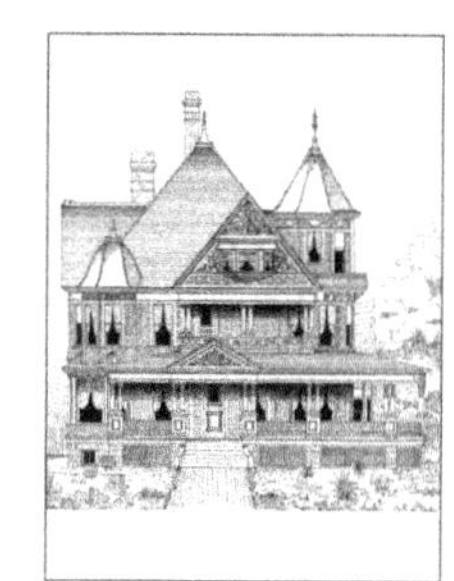

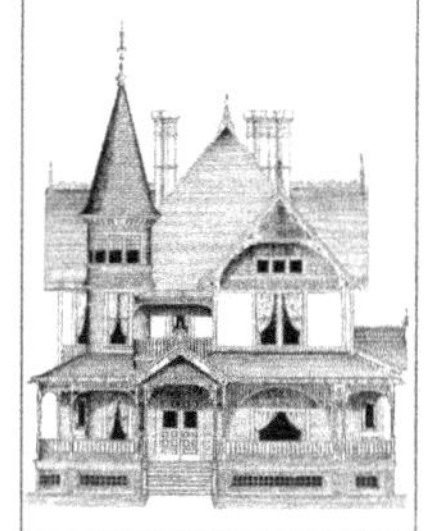

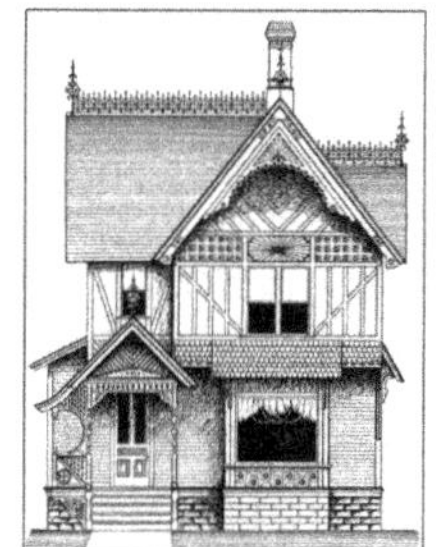

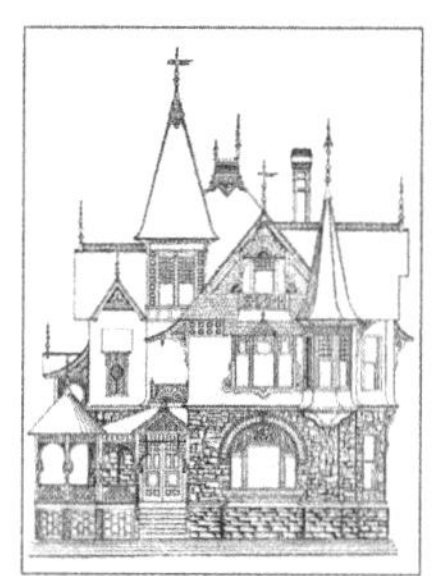

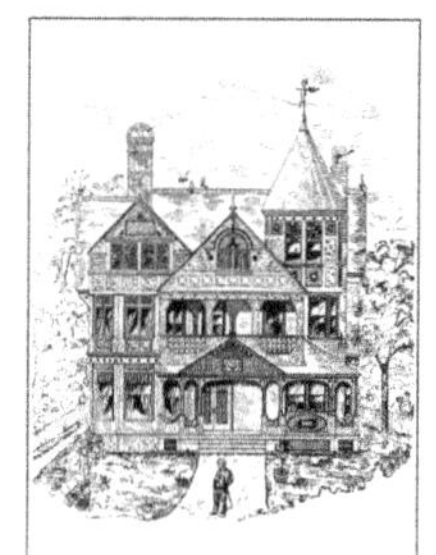

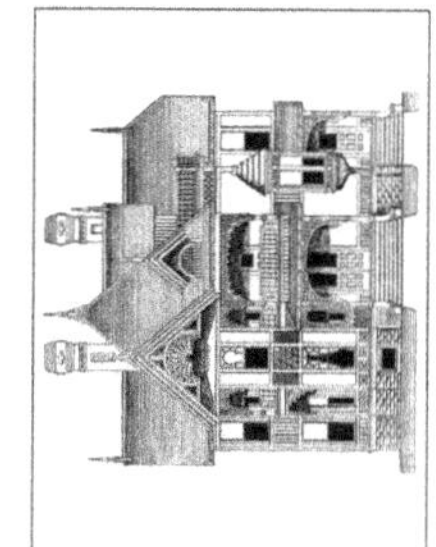

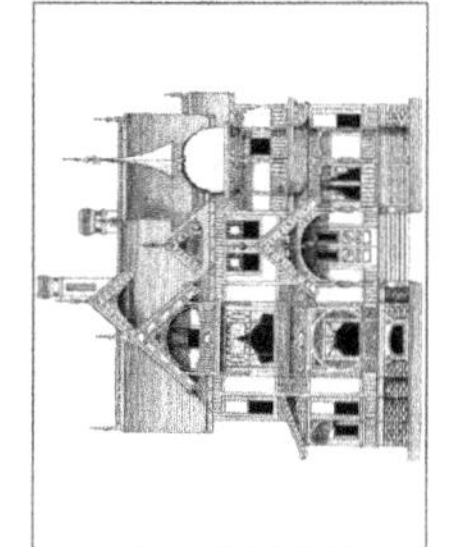

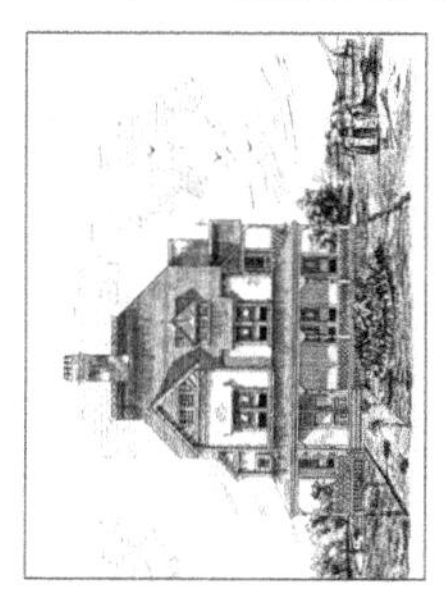

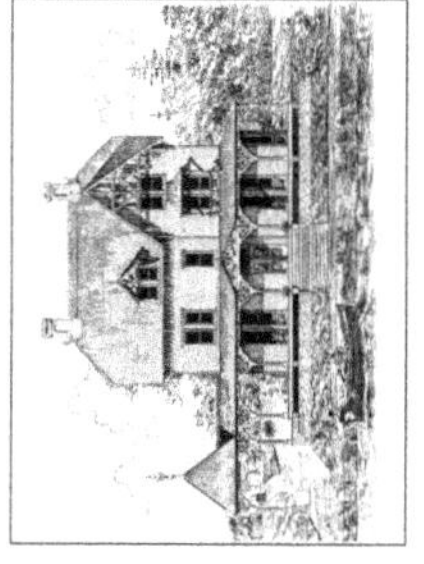

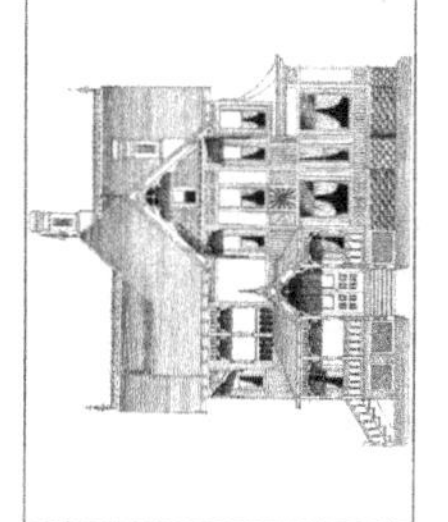

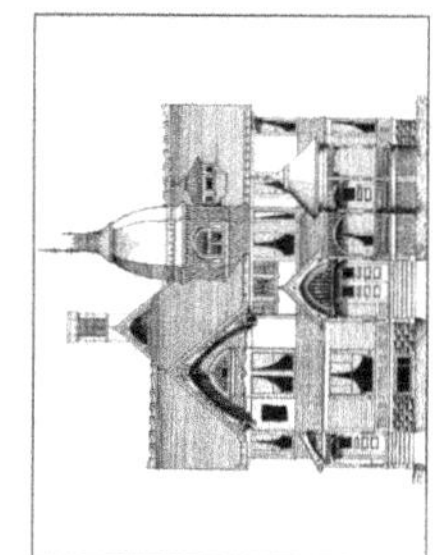

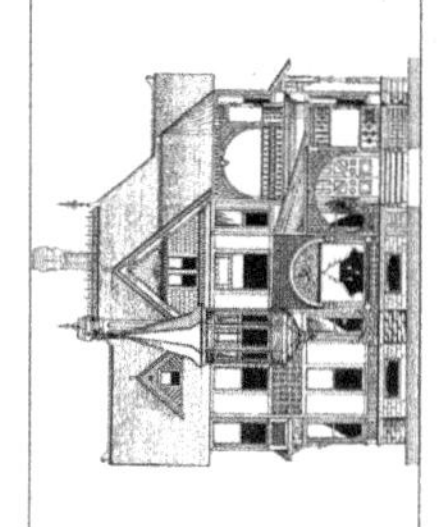

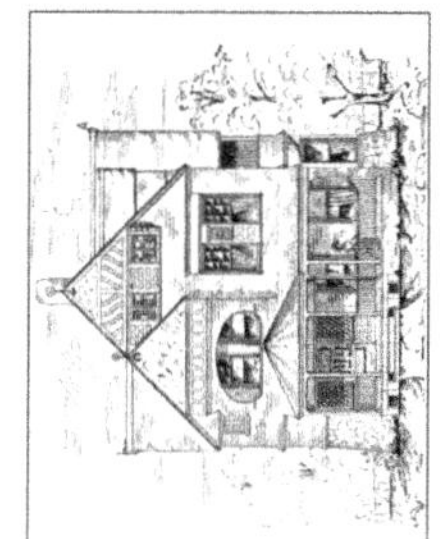

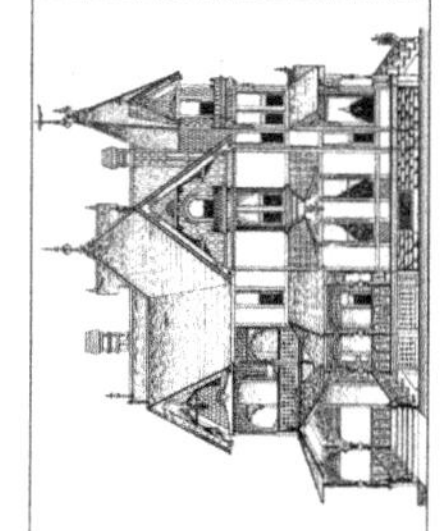

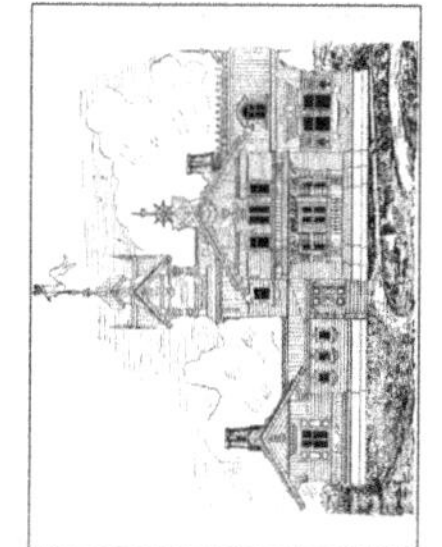

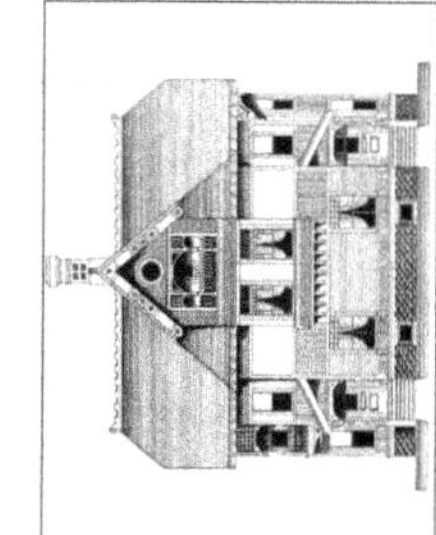

Color & Medium Testing Pages

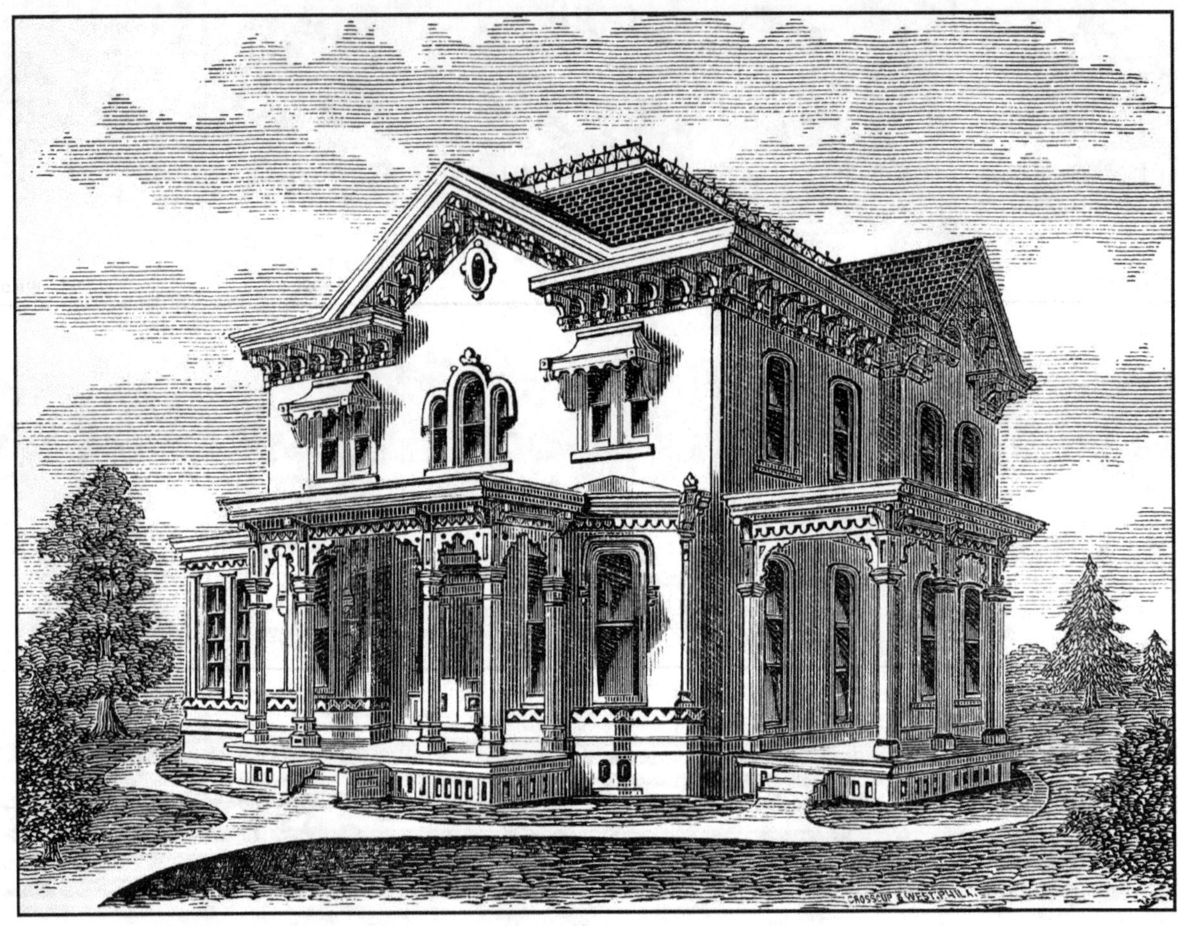

The image above is a reduced-size version of a drawing from the book
Vintage Homes: Adult Coloring Book: Luxurious Victorian Houses & Mansions

Try out your pens, pencils or paints here to get a feel for how they will look on this paper

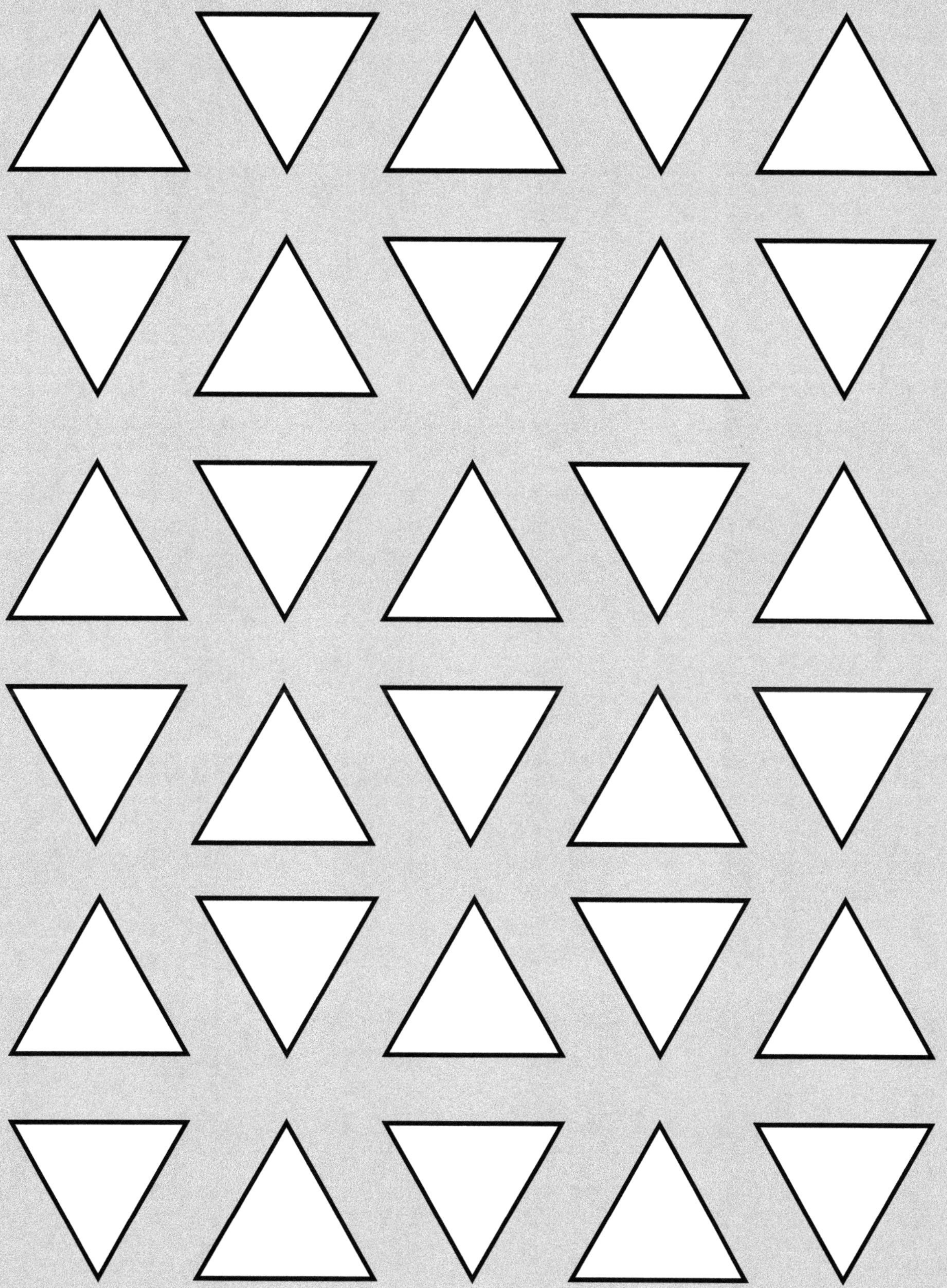

WELCOME!

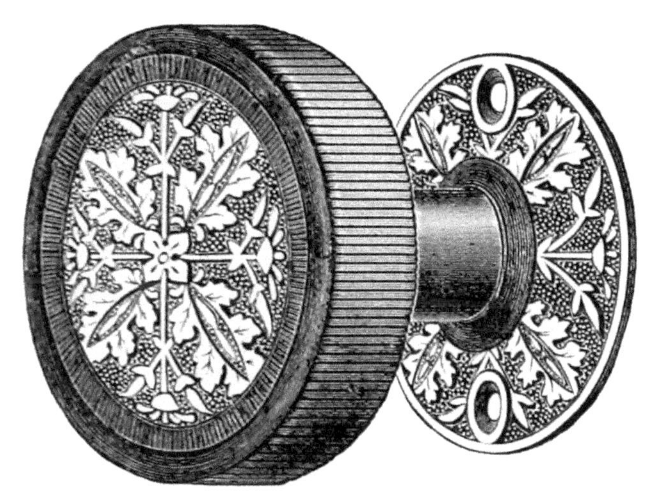

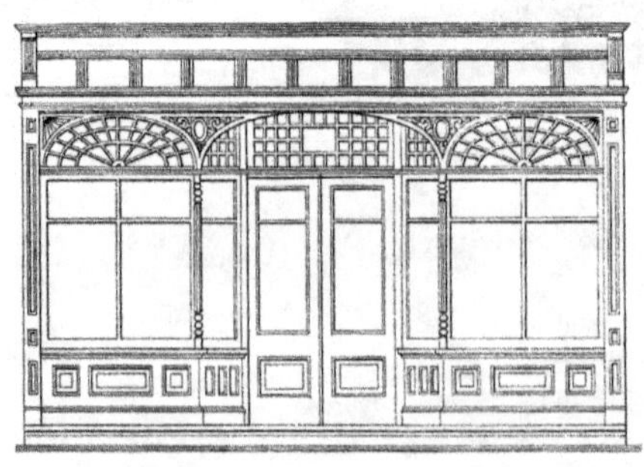

Tip: Find the details about the following illustrations on the back of each page.

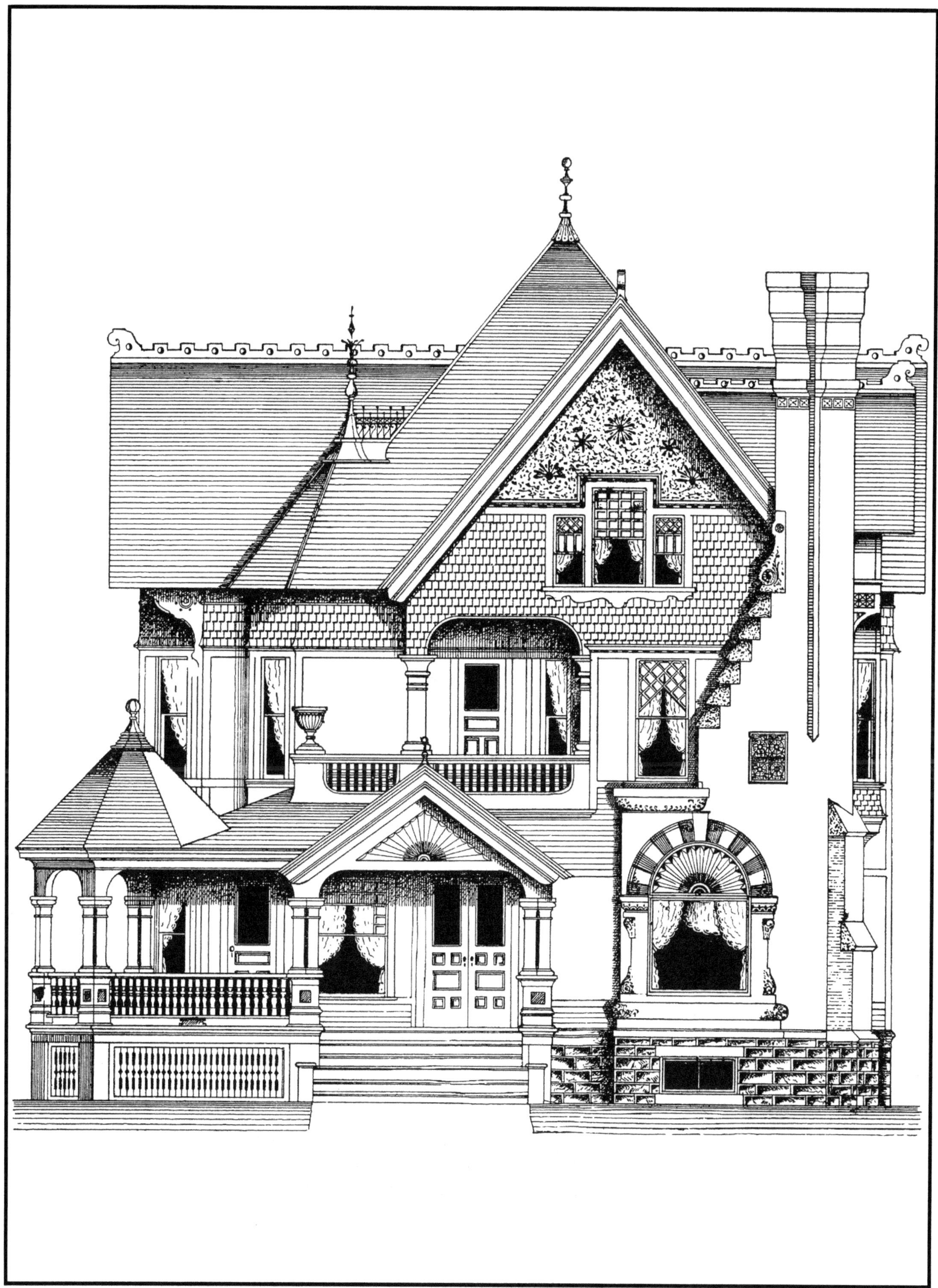

About the illustration on the reverse of this page:

From *The Cottage Souvenir Fourth Edition, Revised* (1896)
by George F. Barber, Architect
Published by Geo. F. Barber & Co., Knoxville, Tennessee

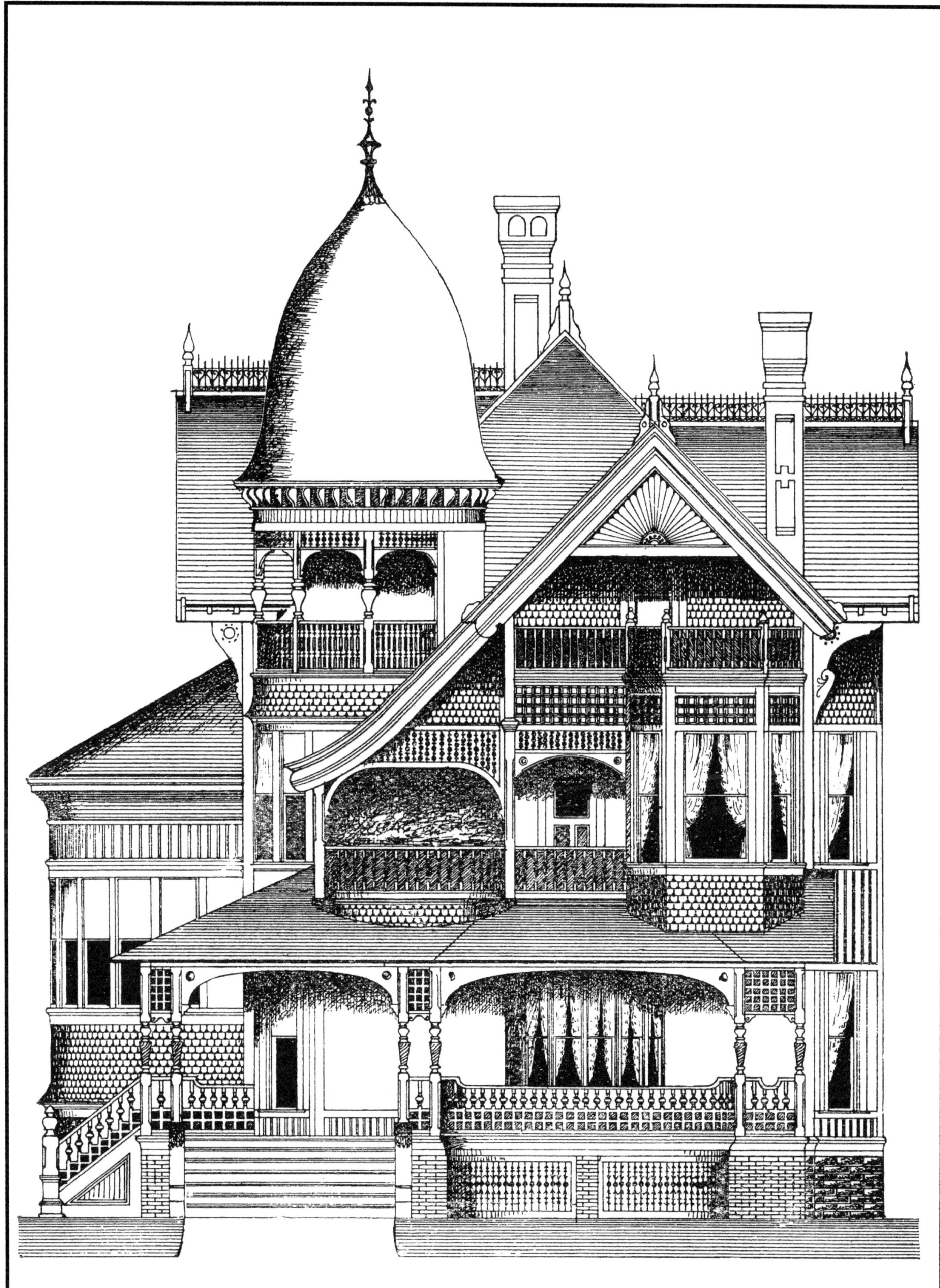

About the illustration on the reverse of this page:

From *The Cottage Souvenir No. 2* (1891)
by George F. Barber, Architect
Published by Geo. F. Barber & Co., Knoxville, Tennessee

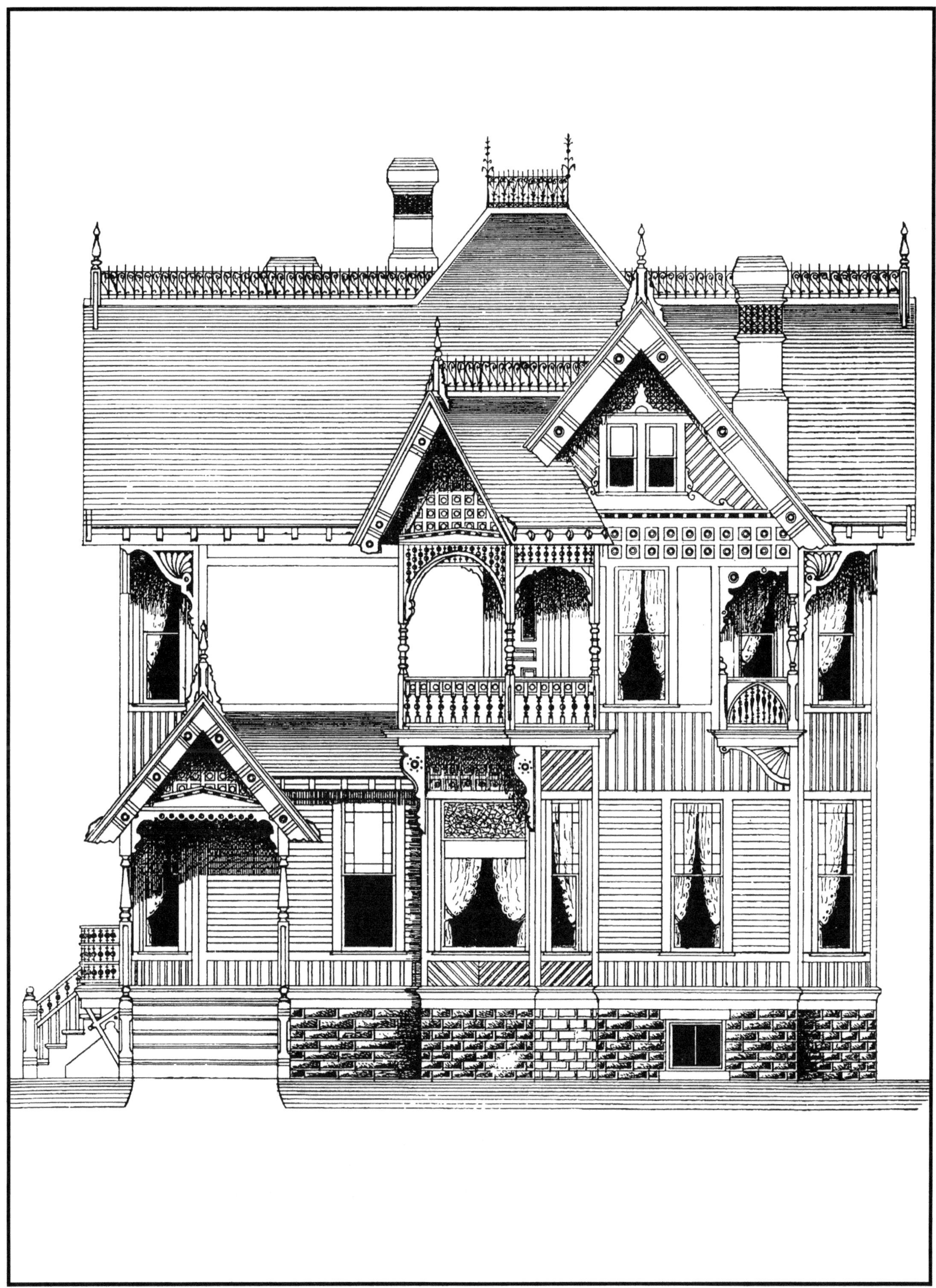

About the illustration on the reverse of this page:

From *The Cottage Souvenir No. 2* (1891)
by George F. Barber, Architect
Published by Geo. F. Barber & Co., Knoxville, Tennessee

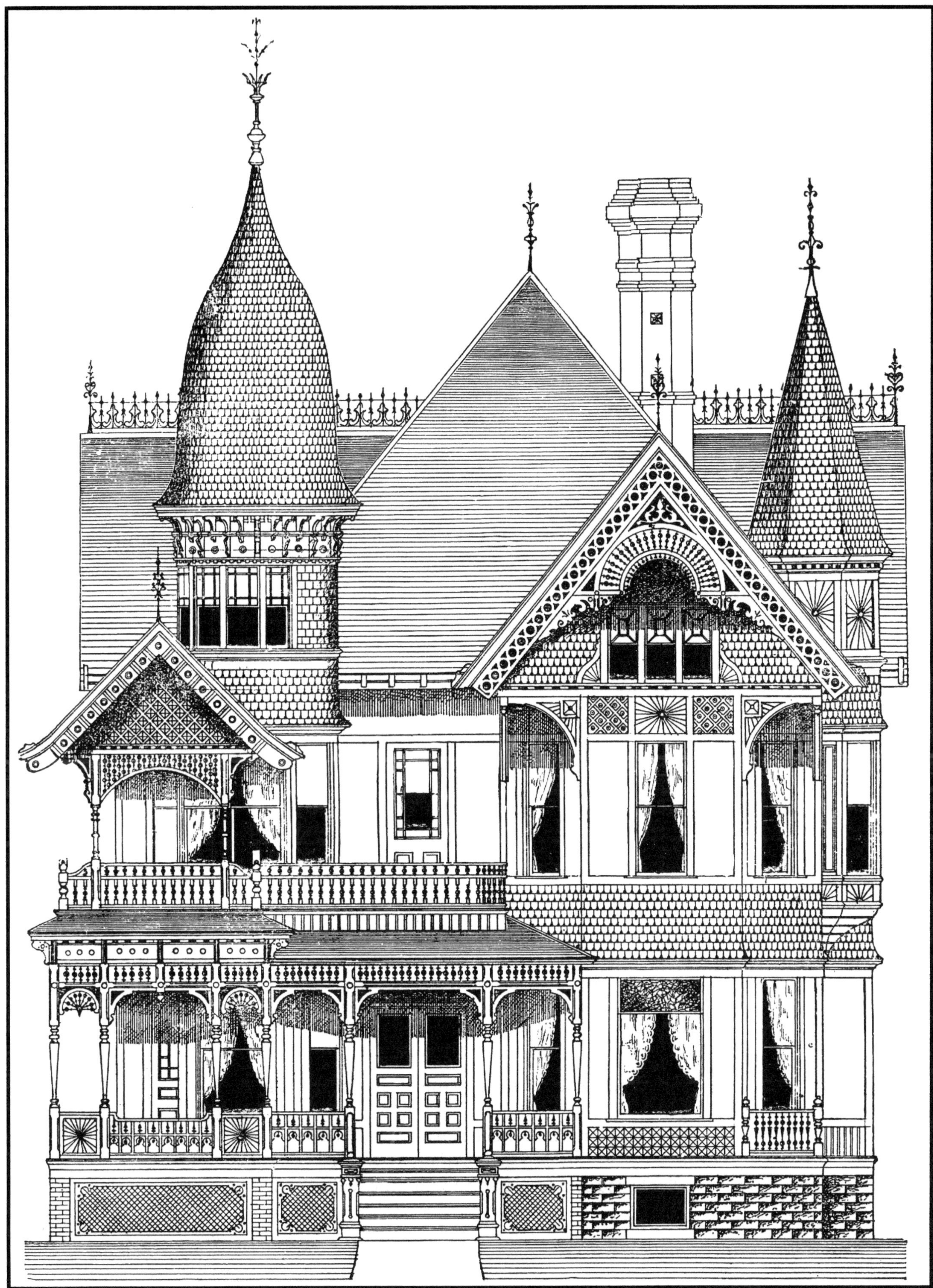

About the illustration on the reverse of this page:

From *The Cottage Souvenir No. 2* (1891)
by George F. Barber, Architect
Published by Geo. F. Barber & Co., Knoxville, Tennessee

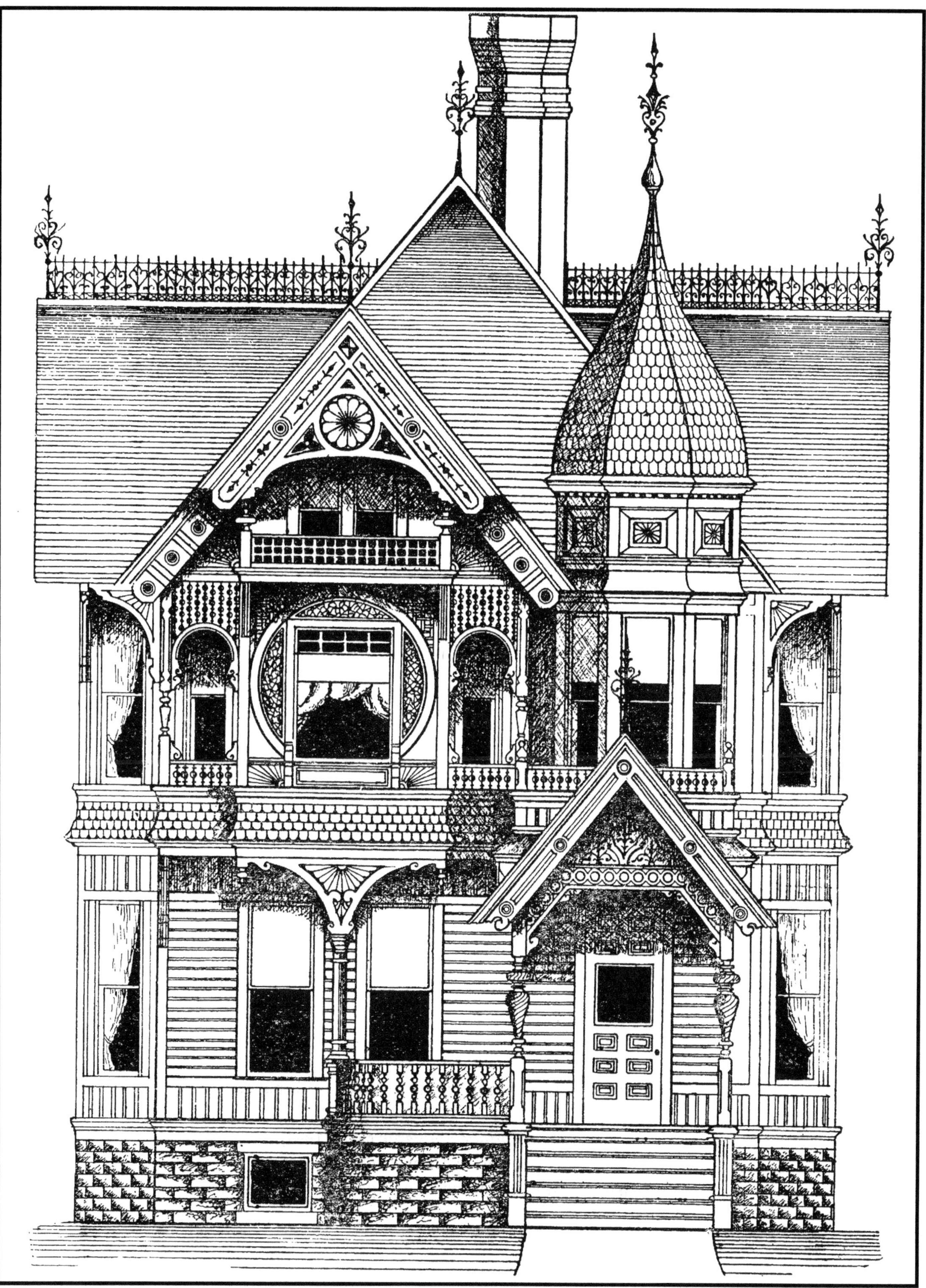

About the illustration on the reverse of this page:

From *The Cottage Souvenir No. 2* (1891)
by George F. Barber, Architect
Published by Geo. F. Barber & Co., Knoxville, Tennessee

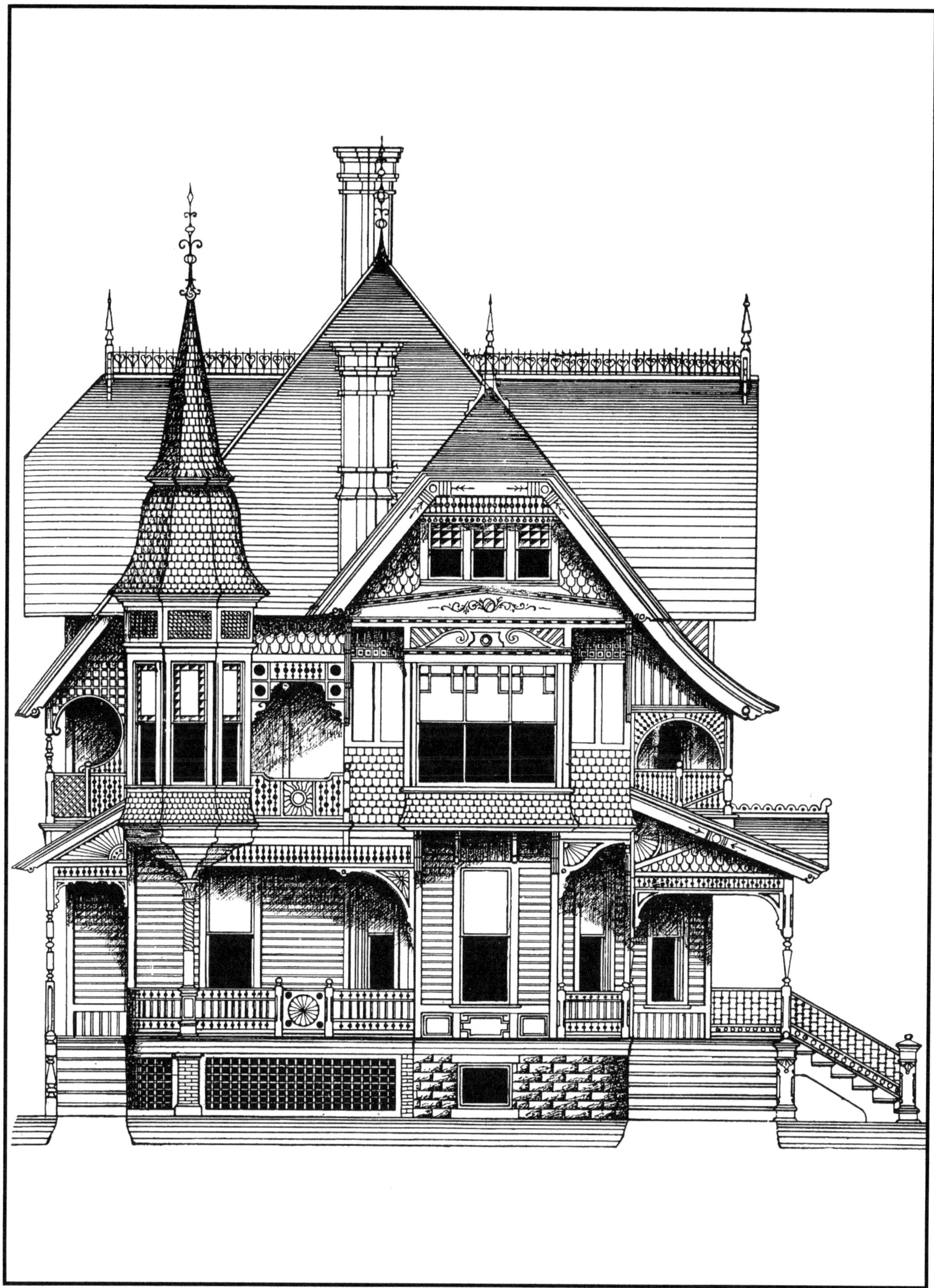

About the illustration on the reverse of this page:

From *The Cottage Souvenir No. 2* (1891)
by George F. Barber, Architect
Published by Geo. F. Barber & Co., Knoxville, Tennessee

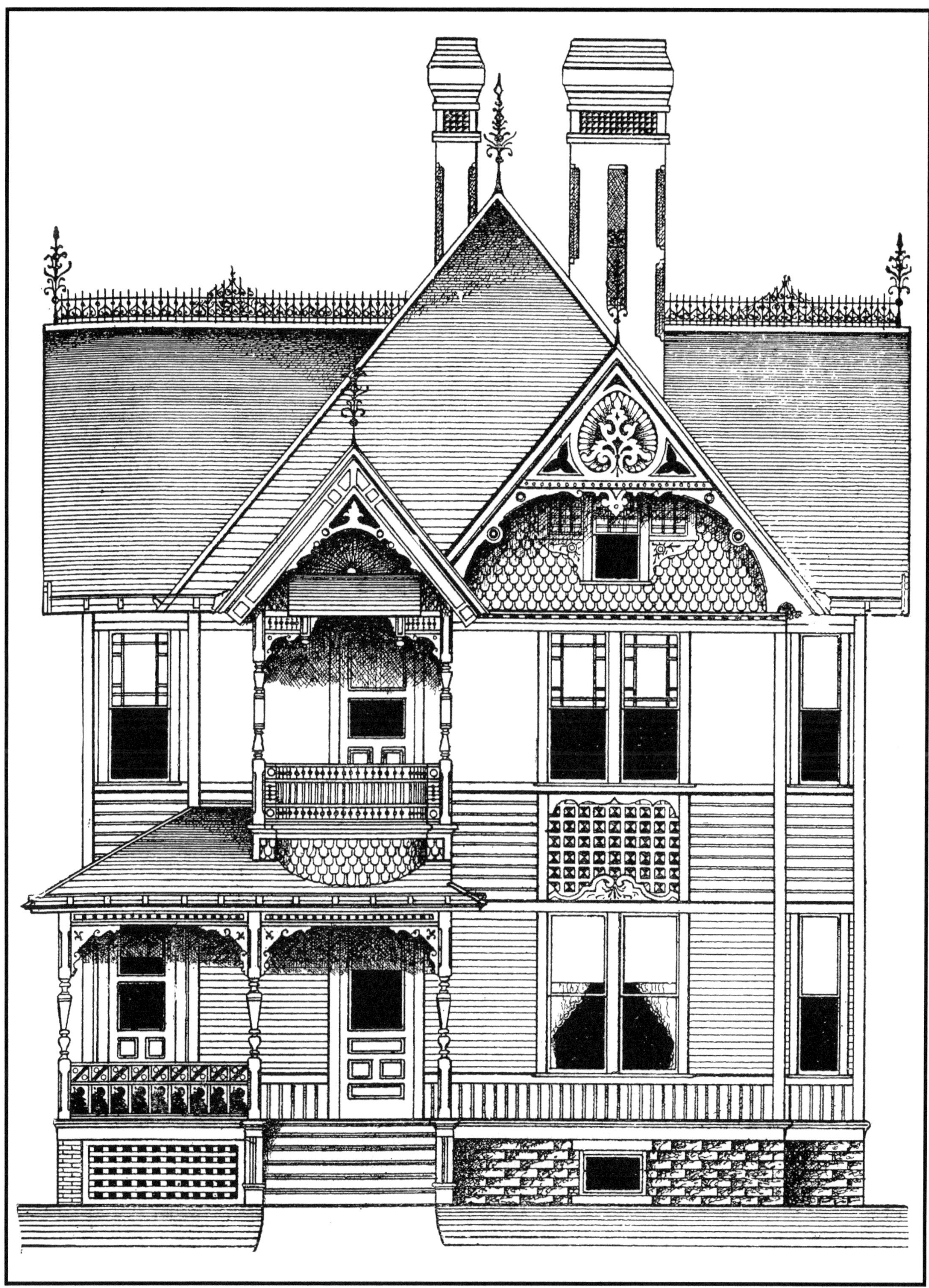

About the illustration on the reverse of this page:

From *The Cottage Souvenir No. 2* (1891)
by George F. Barber, Architect
Published by Geo. F. Barber & Co., Knoxville, Tennessee

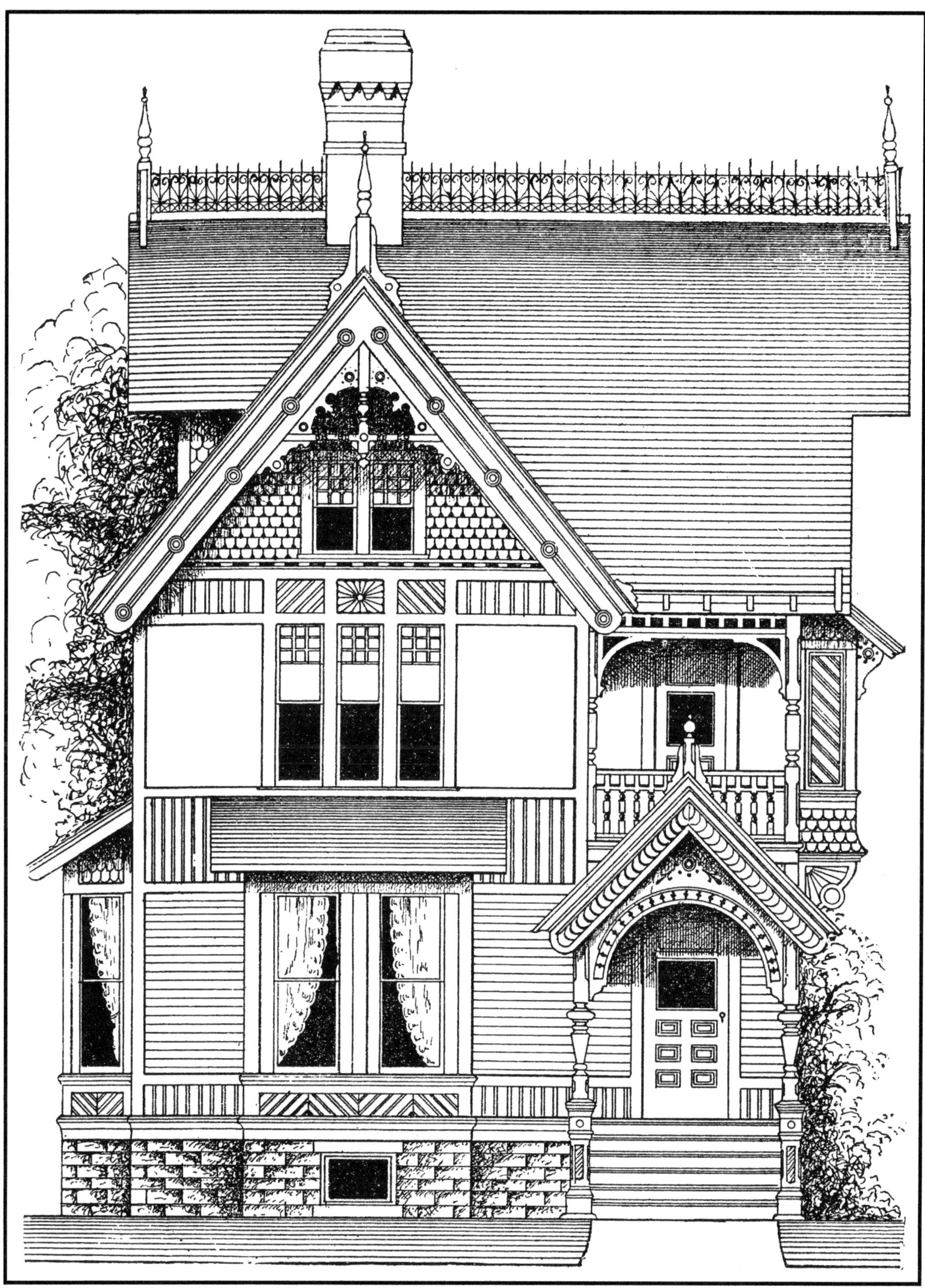

About the illustration on the reverse of this page:

From *The Cottage Souvenir No. 2* (1891)
by George F. Barber, Architect
Published by Geo. F. Barber & Co., Knoxville, Tennessee

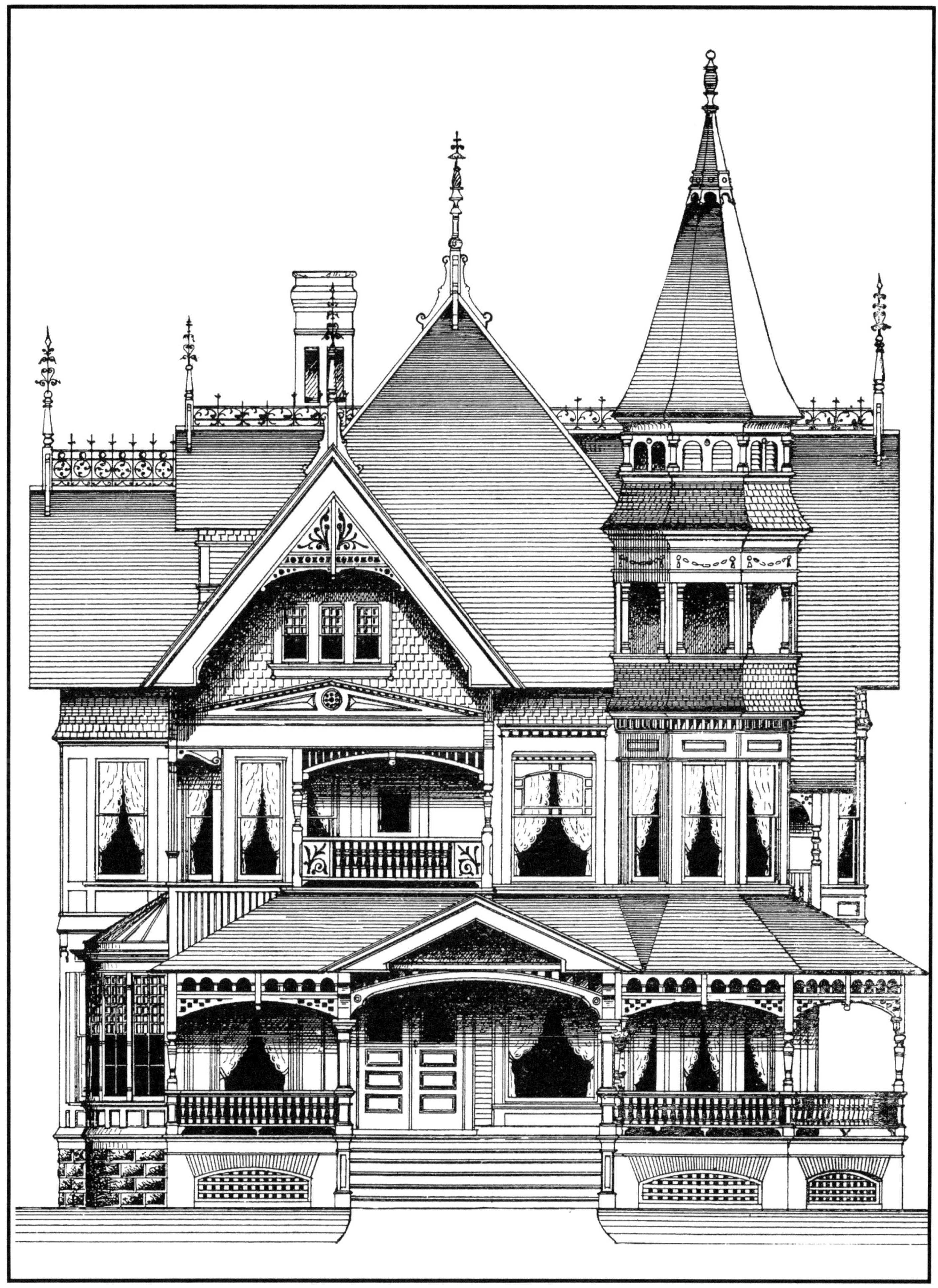

About the illustration on the reverse of this page:

From *The Cottage Souvenir No. 2* (1891)
by George F. Barber, Architect
Published by Geo. F. Barber & Co., Knoxville, Tennessee

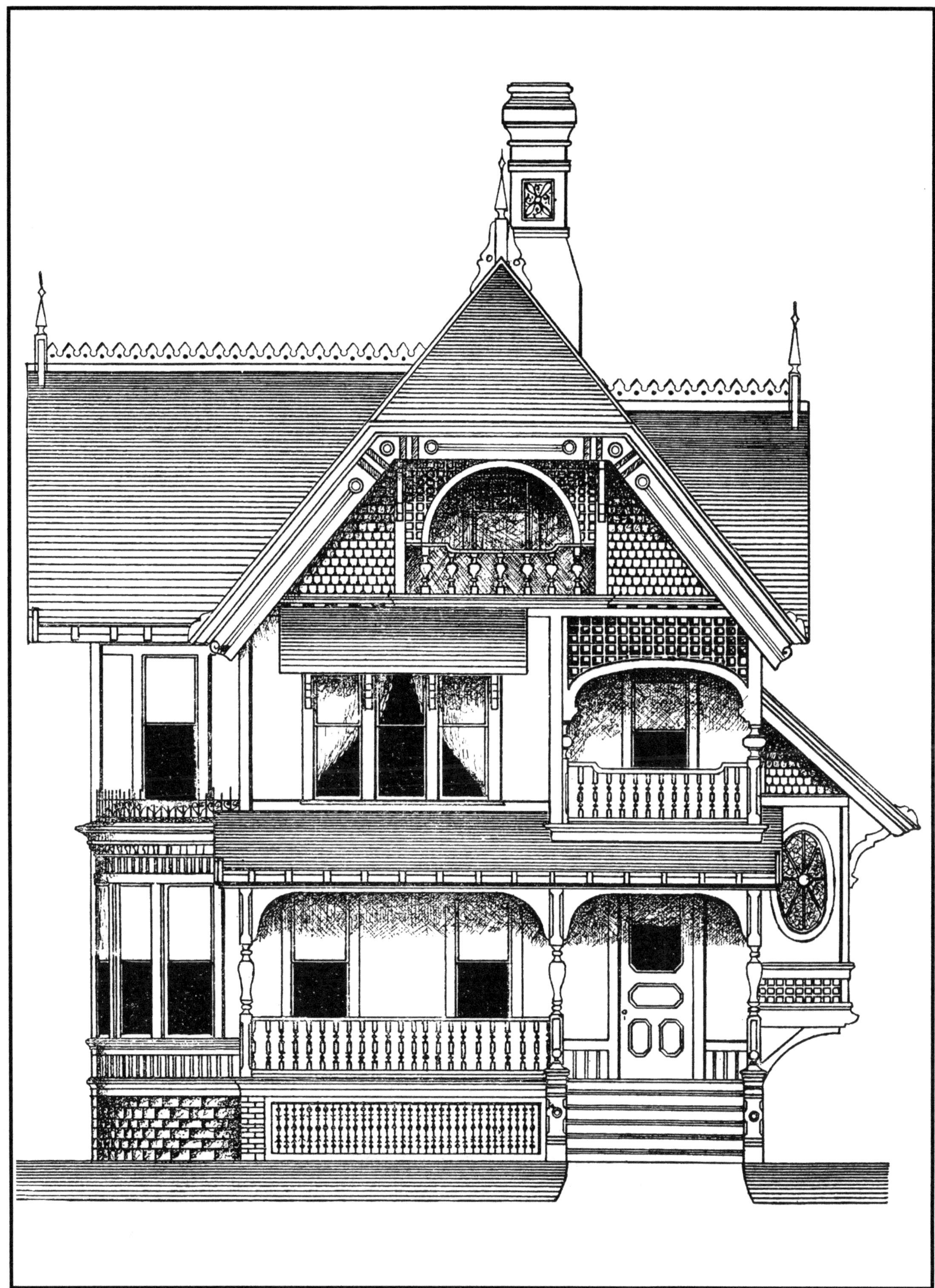

About the illustration on the reverse of this page:

From *The Cottage Souvenir No. 2* (1891)
by George F. Barber, Architect
Published by Geo. F. Barber & Co., Knoxville, Tennessee

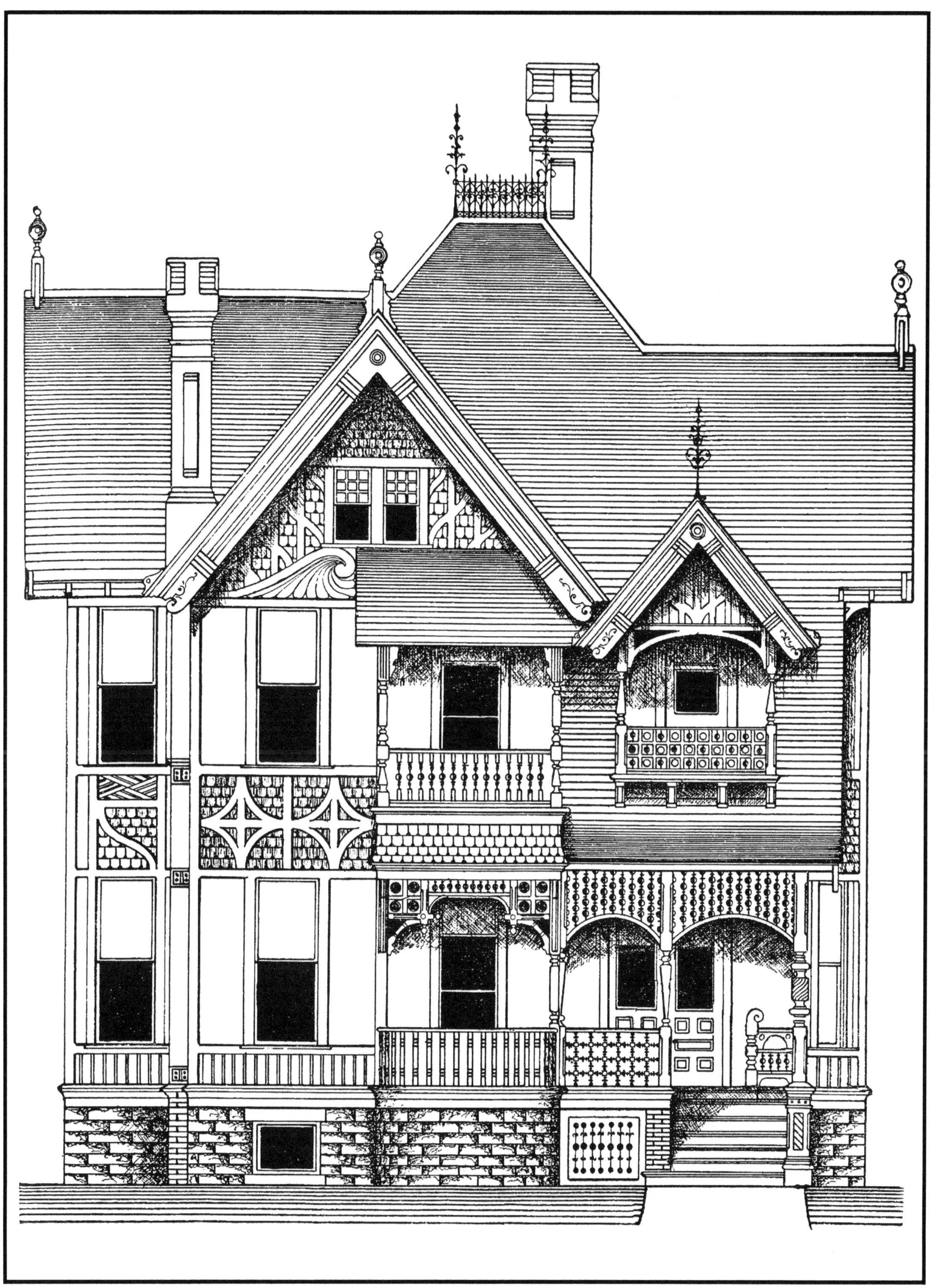

About the illustration on the reverse of this page:

From *The Cottage Souvenir No. 2* (1891)
by George F. Barber, Architect
Published by Geo. F. Barber & Co., Knoxville, Tennessee

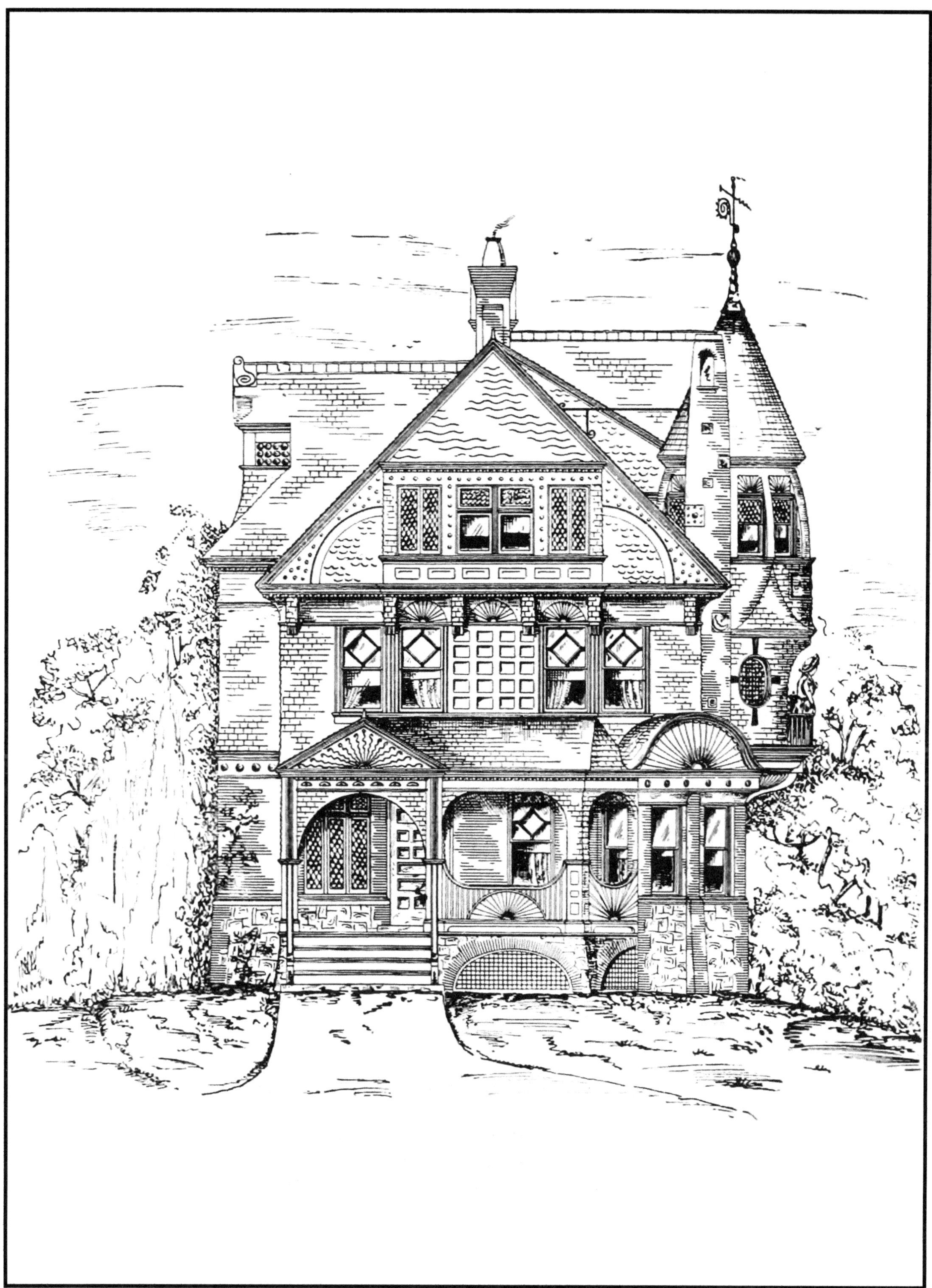

About the illustration on the reverse of this page:

From *Dwellings for Village and Country* (1885)
by Samuel Burrage Reed, Architect
Published by O. Judd Co., New York, New York

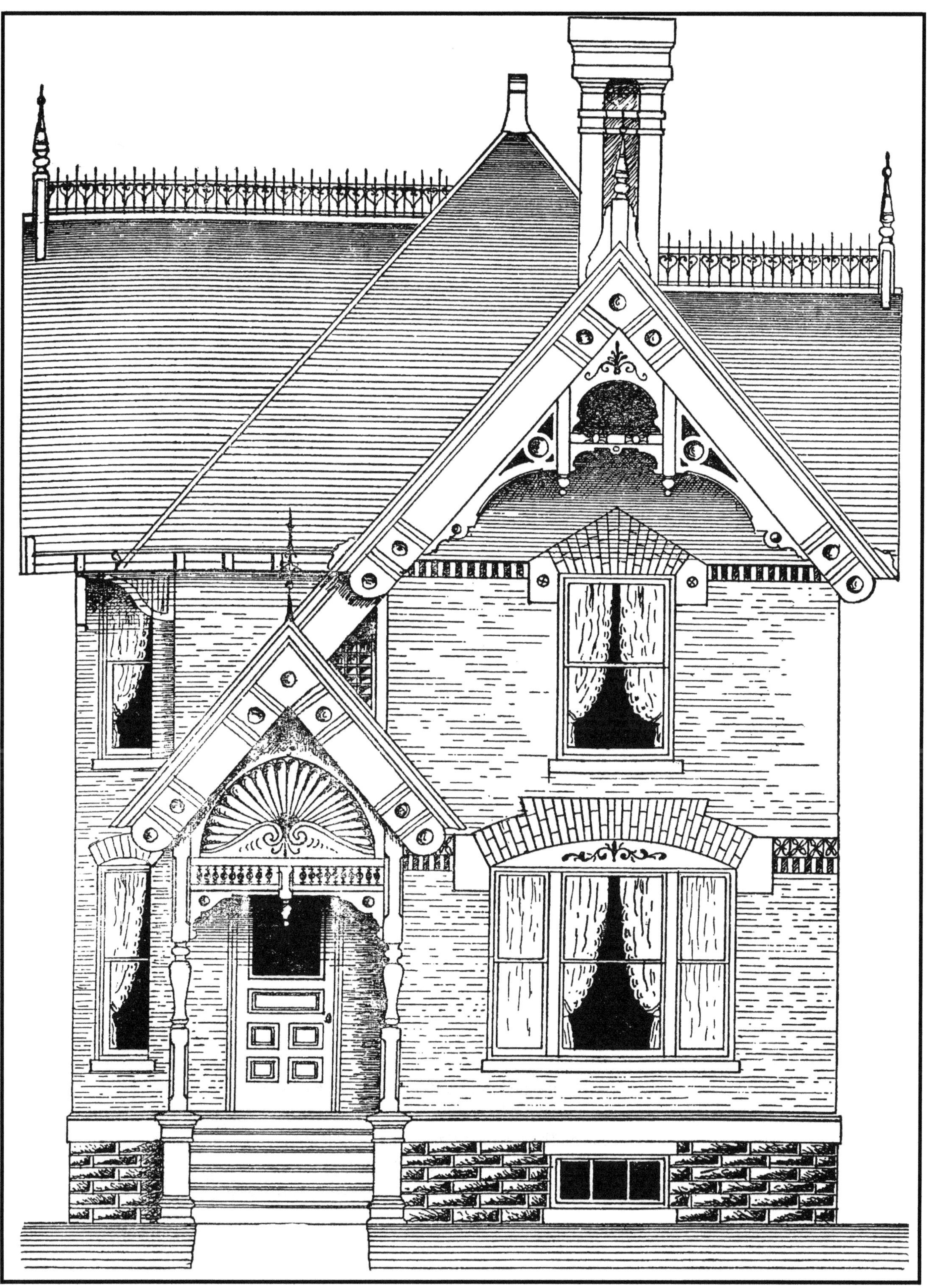

About the illustration on the reverse of this page:

From *The Cottage Souvenir No. 2* (1891)
by George F. Barber, Architect
Published by Geo. F. Barber & Co., Knoxville, Tennessee

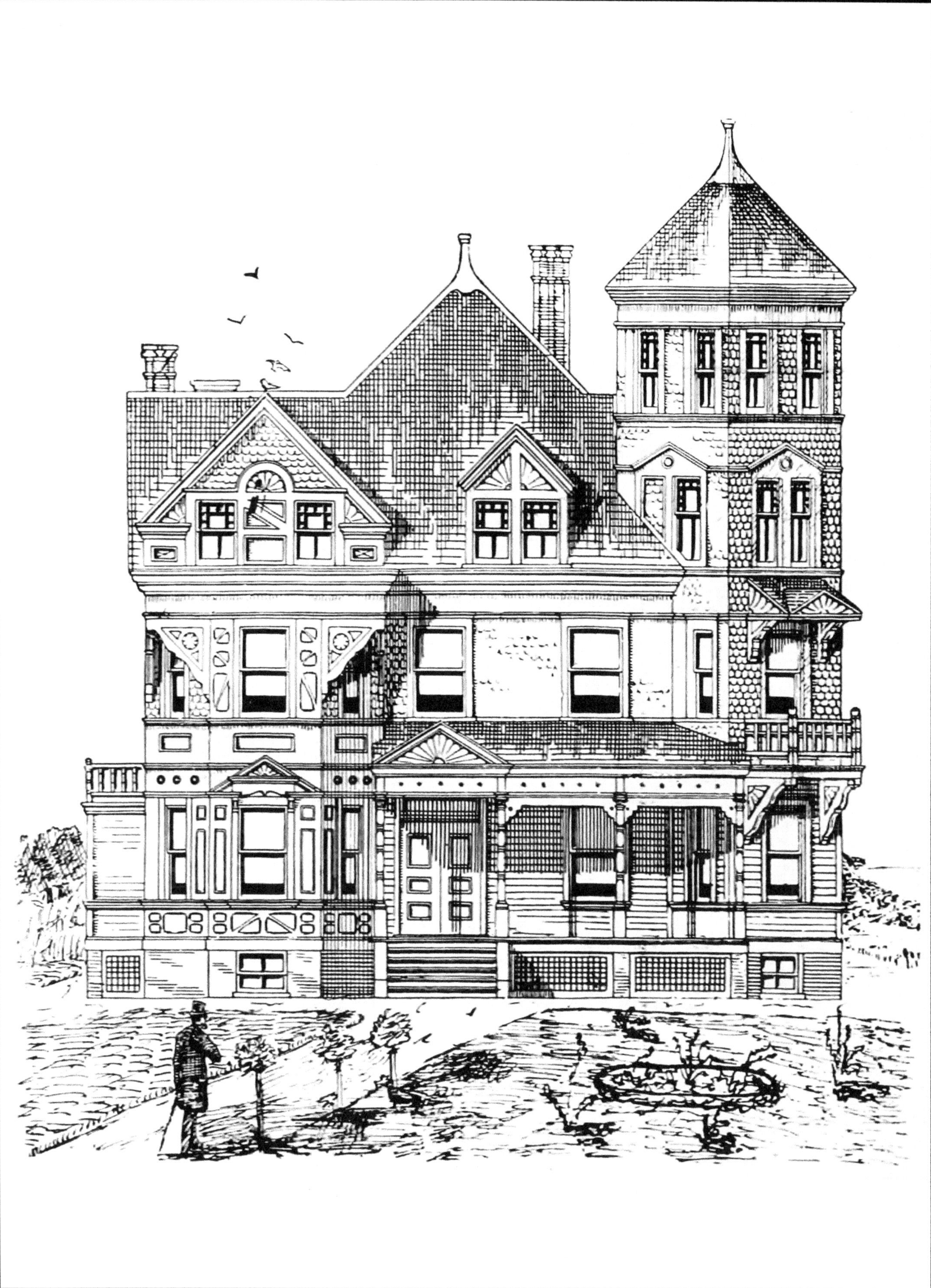

About the illustration on the reverse of this page:

From *Dwellings for Village and Country* (1885)
by Samuel Burrage Reed, Architect
Published by O. Judd Co., New York, New York

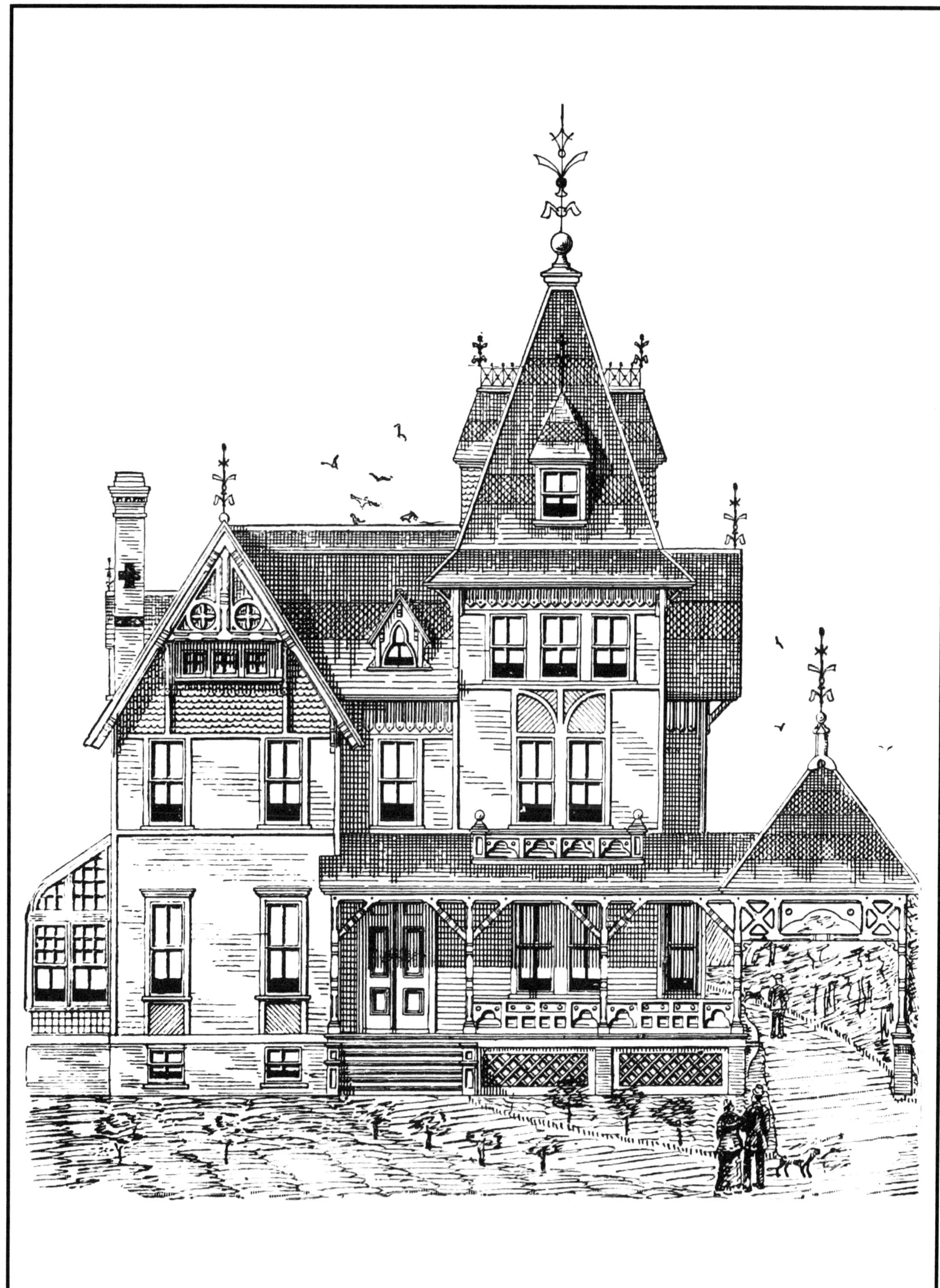

About the illustration on the reverse of this page:

From *Dwellings for Village and Country* (1885)
by Samuel Burrage Reed, Architect
Published by O. Judd Co., New York, New York

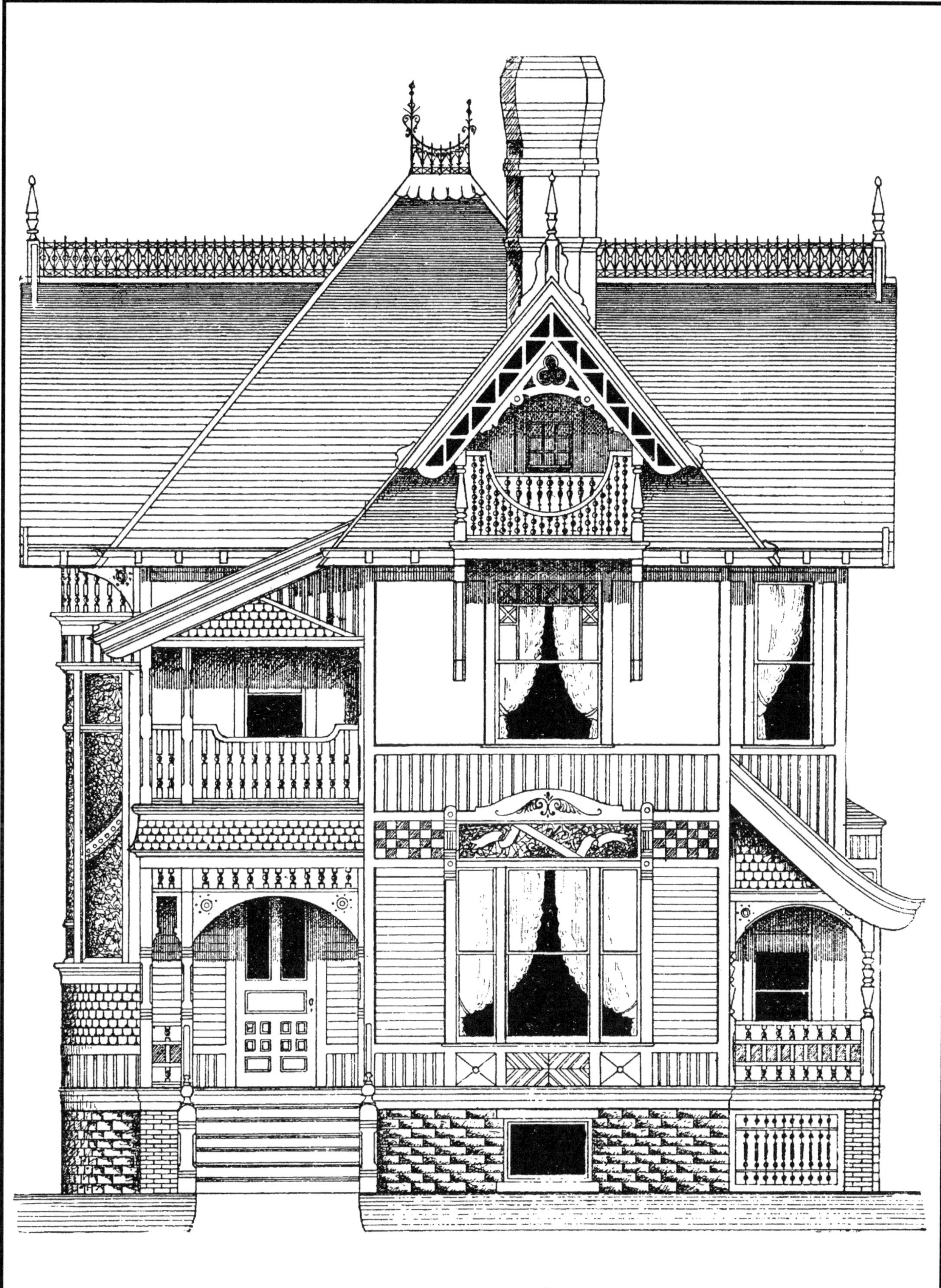

About the illustration on the reverse of this page:

From *The Cottage Souvenir No. 2* (1891)
by George F. Barber, Architect
Published by Geo. F. Barber & Co., Knoxville, Tennessee

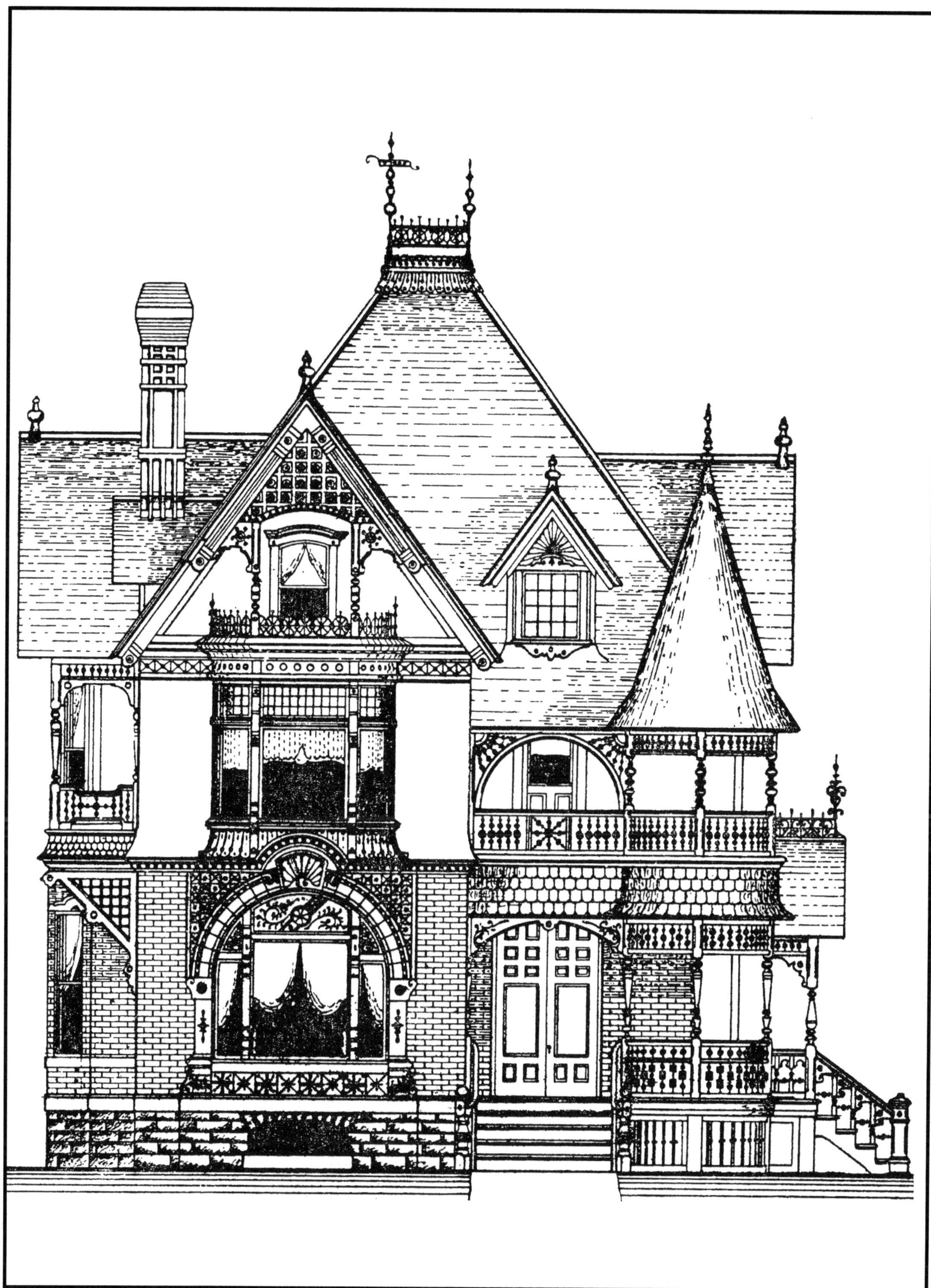

About the illustration on the reverse of this page:

From *The Cottage Souvenir No. 2* (1891)
by George F. Barber, Architect
Published by Geo. F. Barber & Co., Knoxville, Tennessee

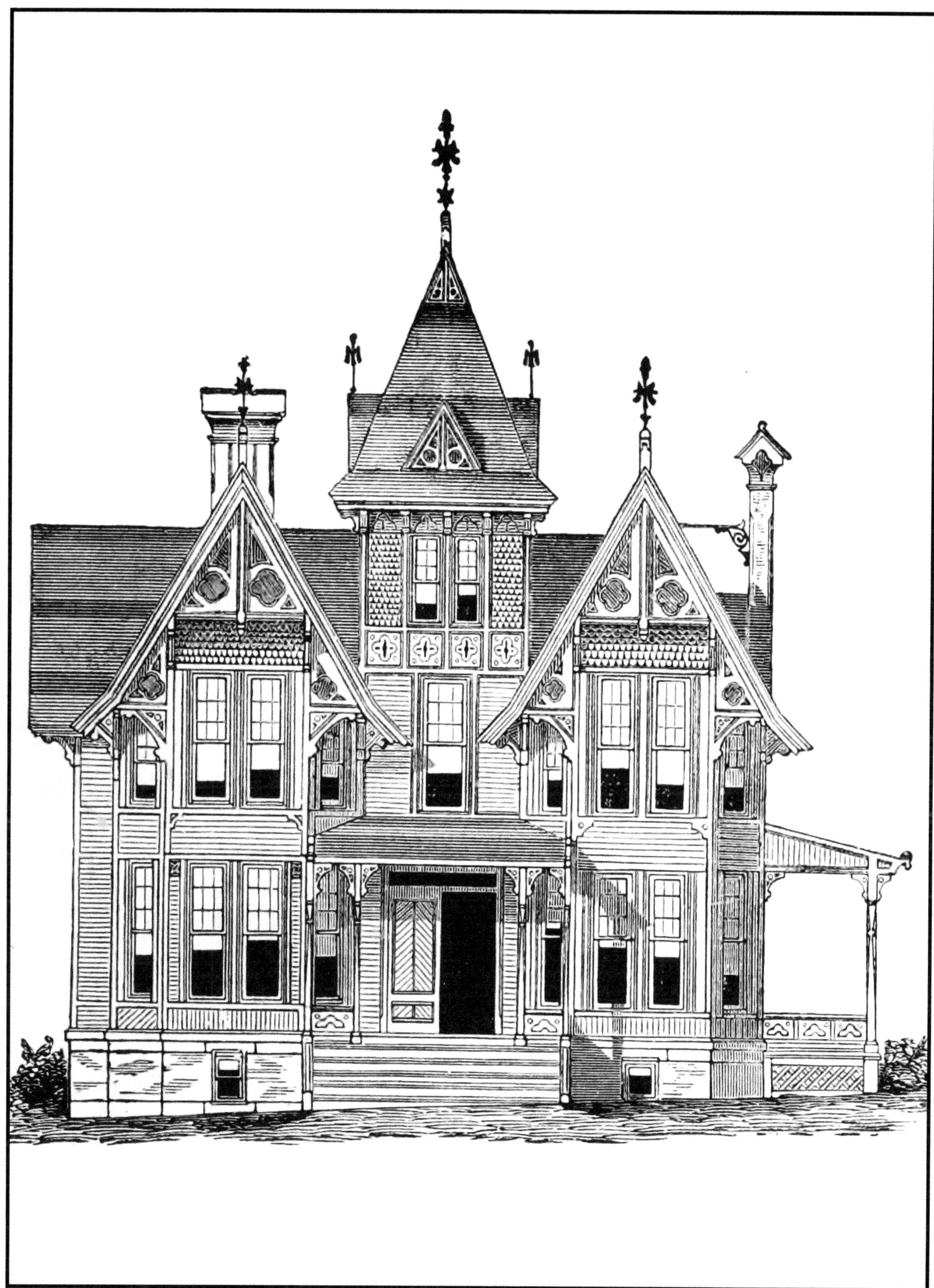

About the illustration on the reverse of this page:

From *Specimen Book of One Hundred Architectural Designs* (1880)
by Bicknell and Comstock
Published by Bicknell & Comstock, New York

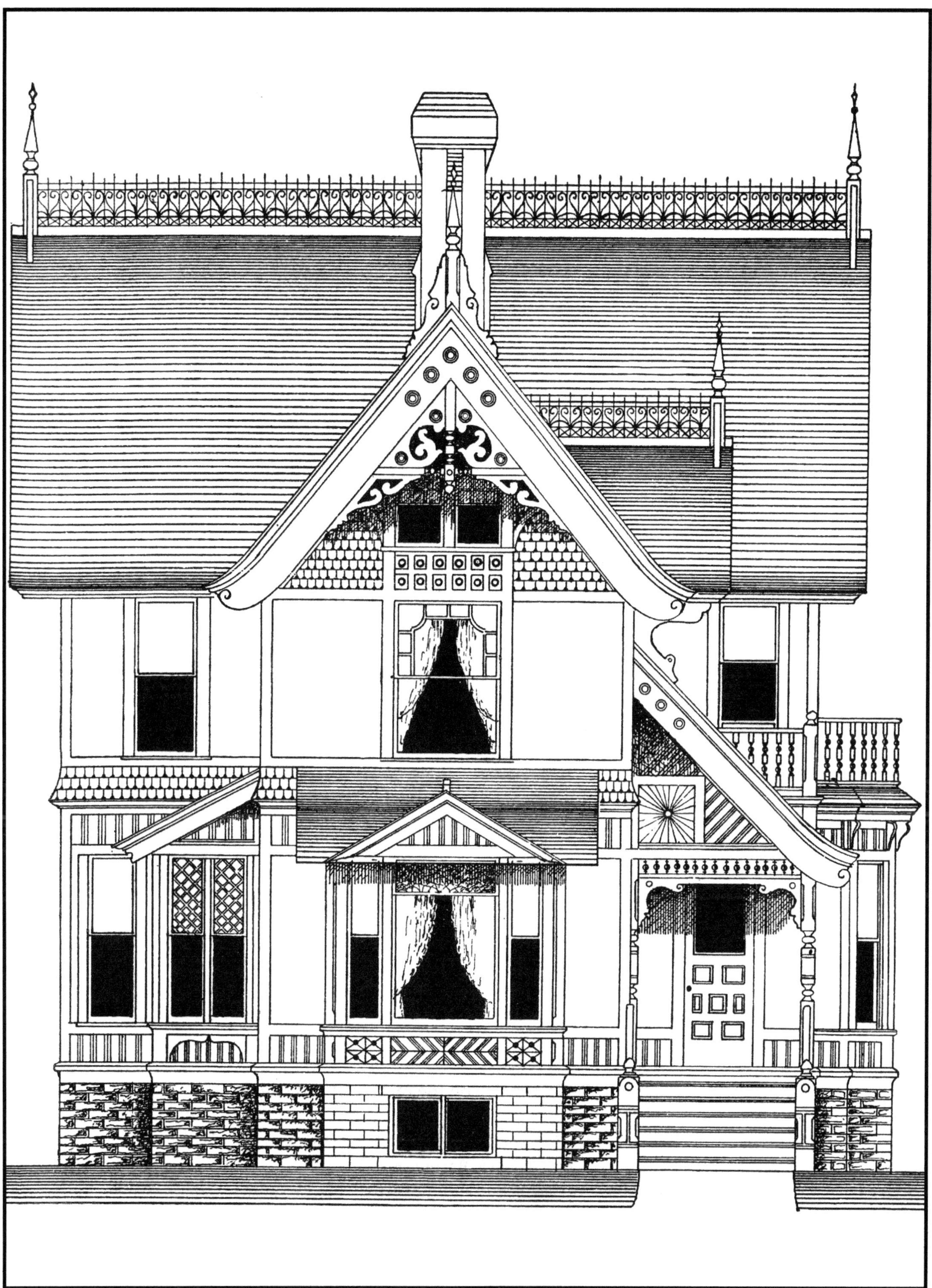

About the illustration on the reverse of this page:

From *The Cottage Souvenir No. 2* (1891)
by George F. Barber, Architect
Published by Geo. F. Barber & Co., Knoxville, Tennessee

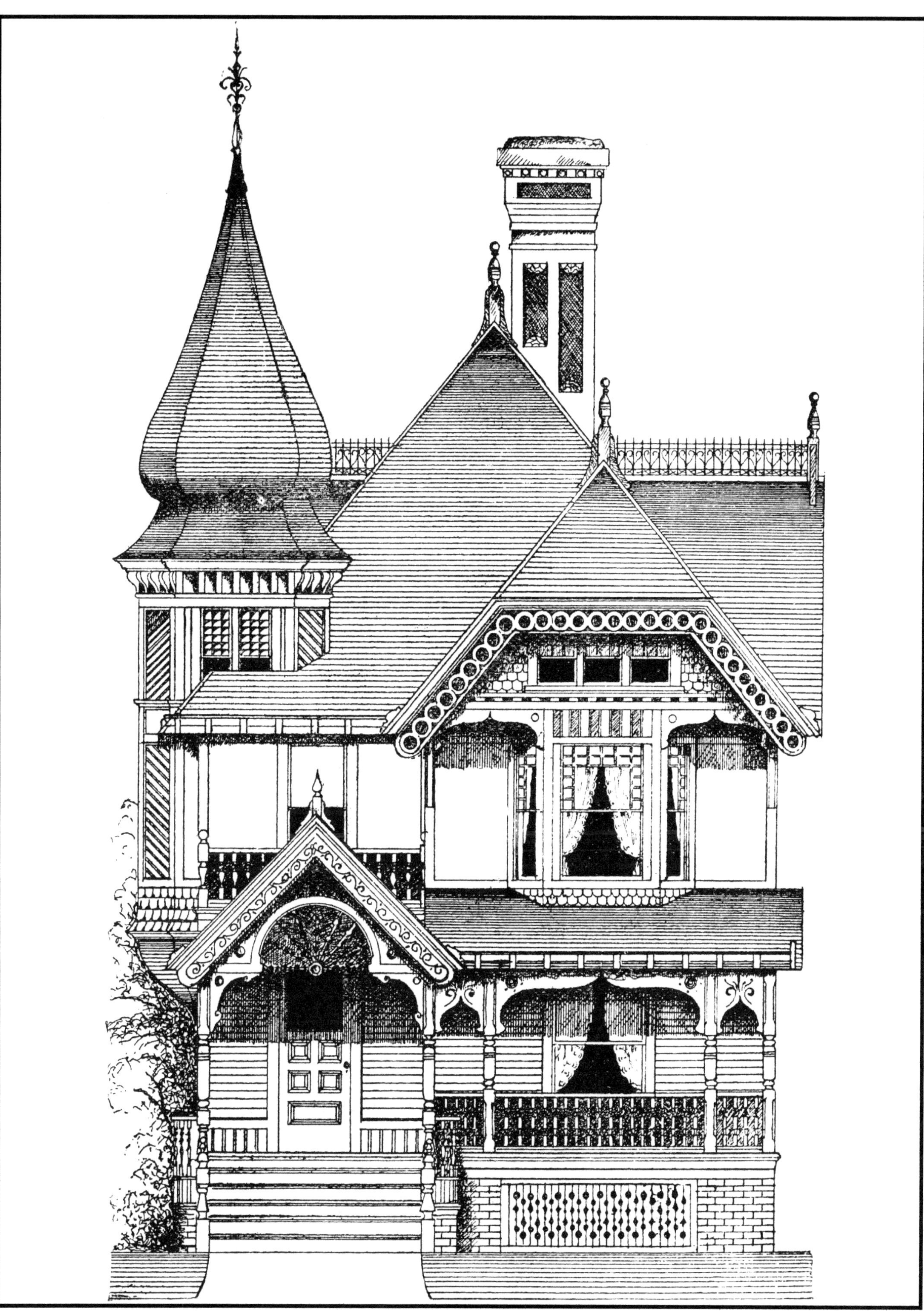

About the illustration on the reverse of this page:

From *The Cottage Souvenir No. 2* (1891)
by George F. Barber, Architect
Published by Geo. F. Barber & Co., Knoxville, Tennessee

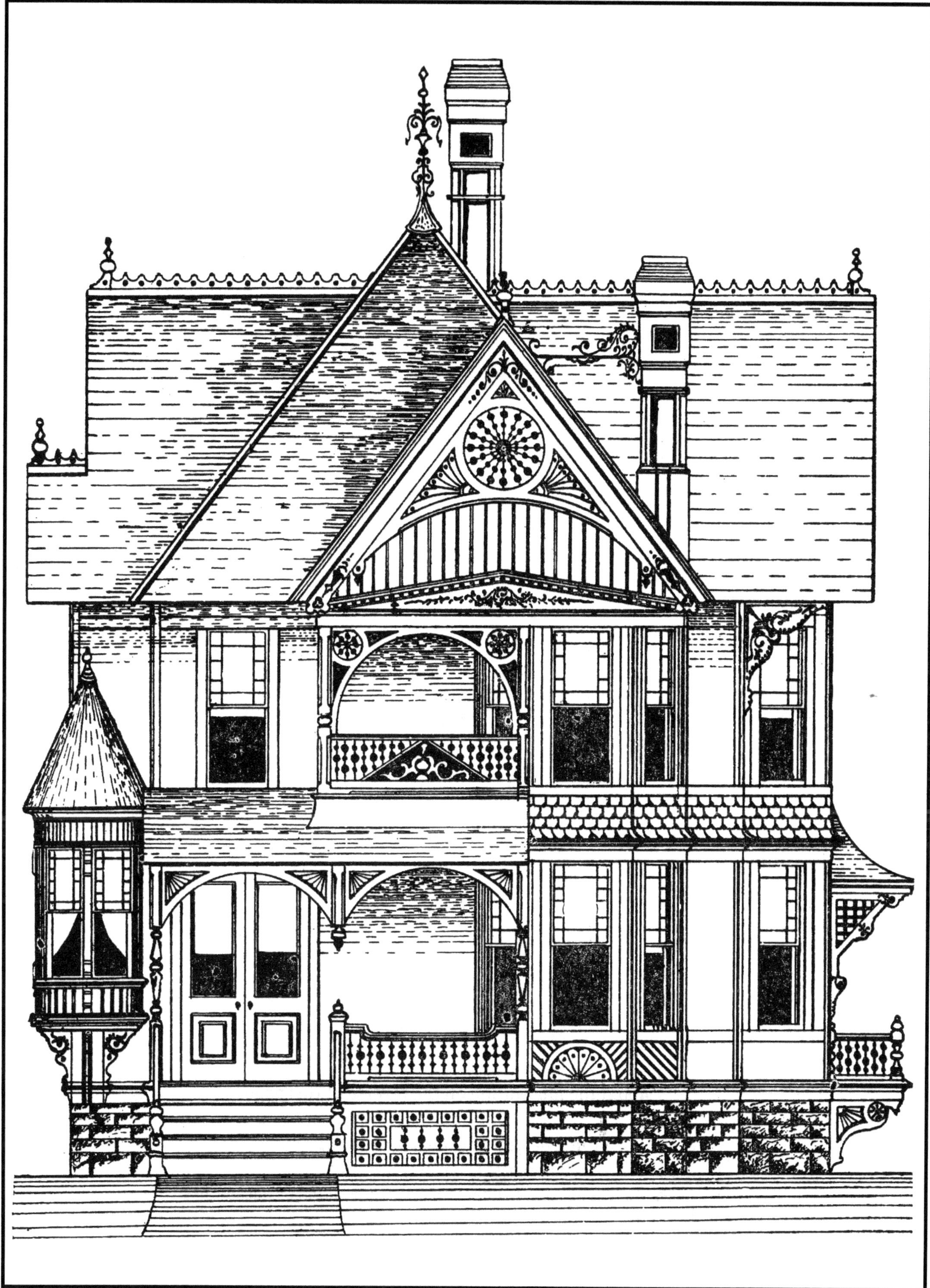

About the illustration on the reverse of this page:

From *The Cottage Souvenir No. 2* (1891)
by George F. Barber, Architect
Published by Geo. F. Barber & Co., Knoxville, Tennessee

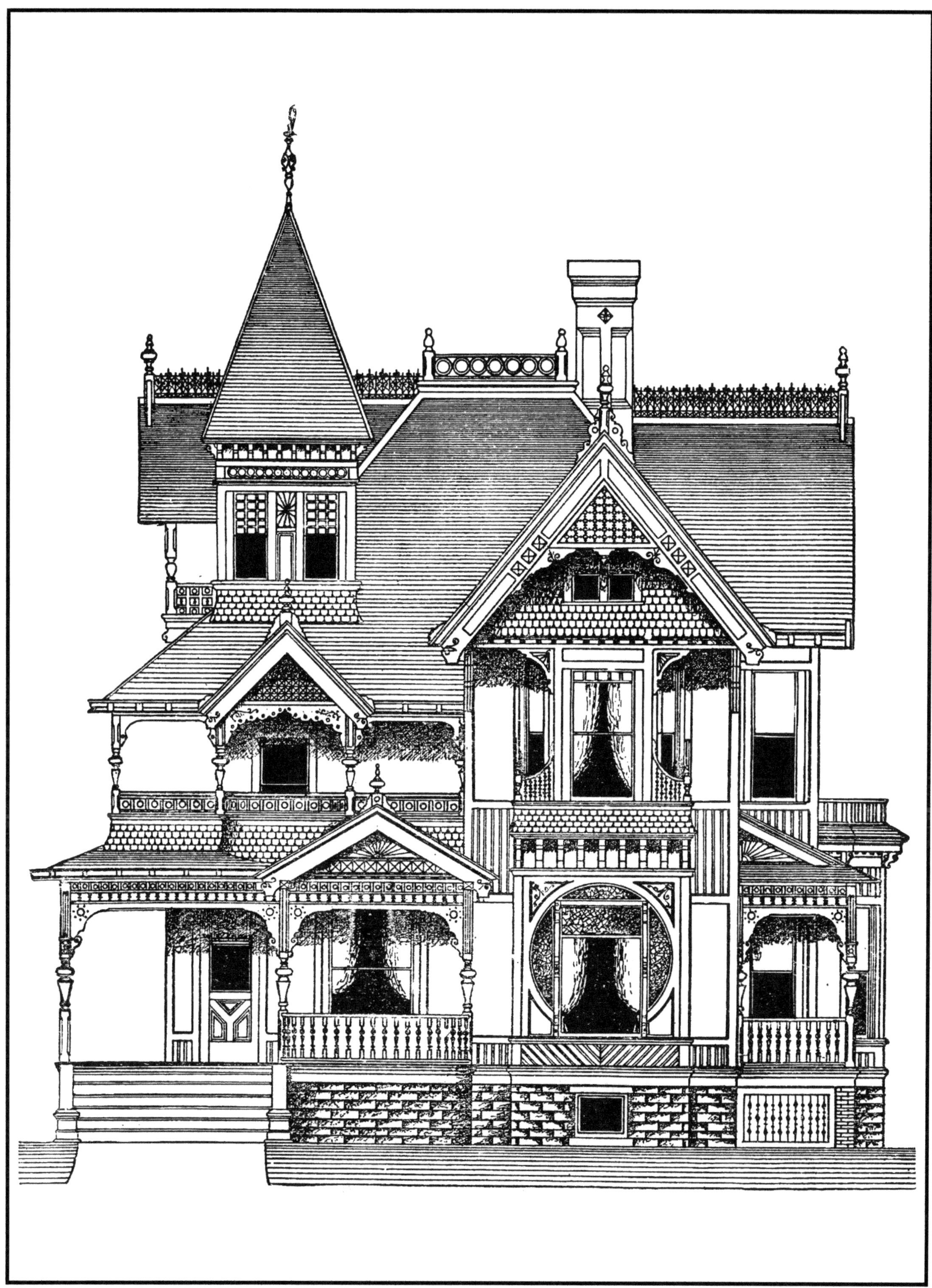

About the illustration on the reverse of this page:

From *The Cottage Souvenir No. 2* (1891)
by George F. Barber, Architect
Published by Geo. F. Barber & Co., Knoxville, Tennessee

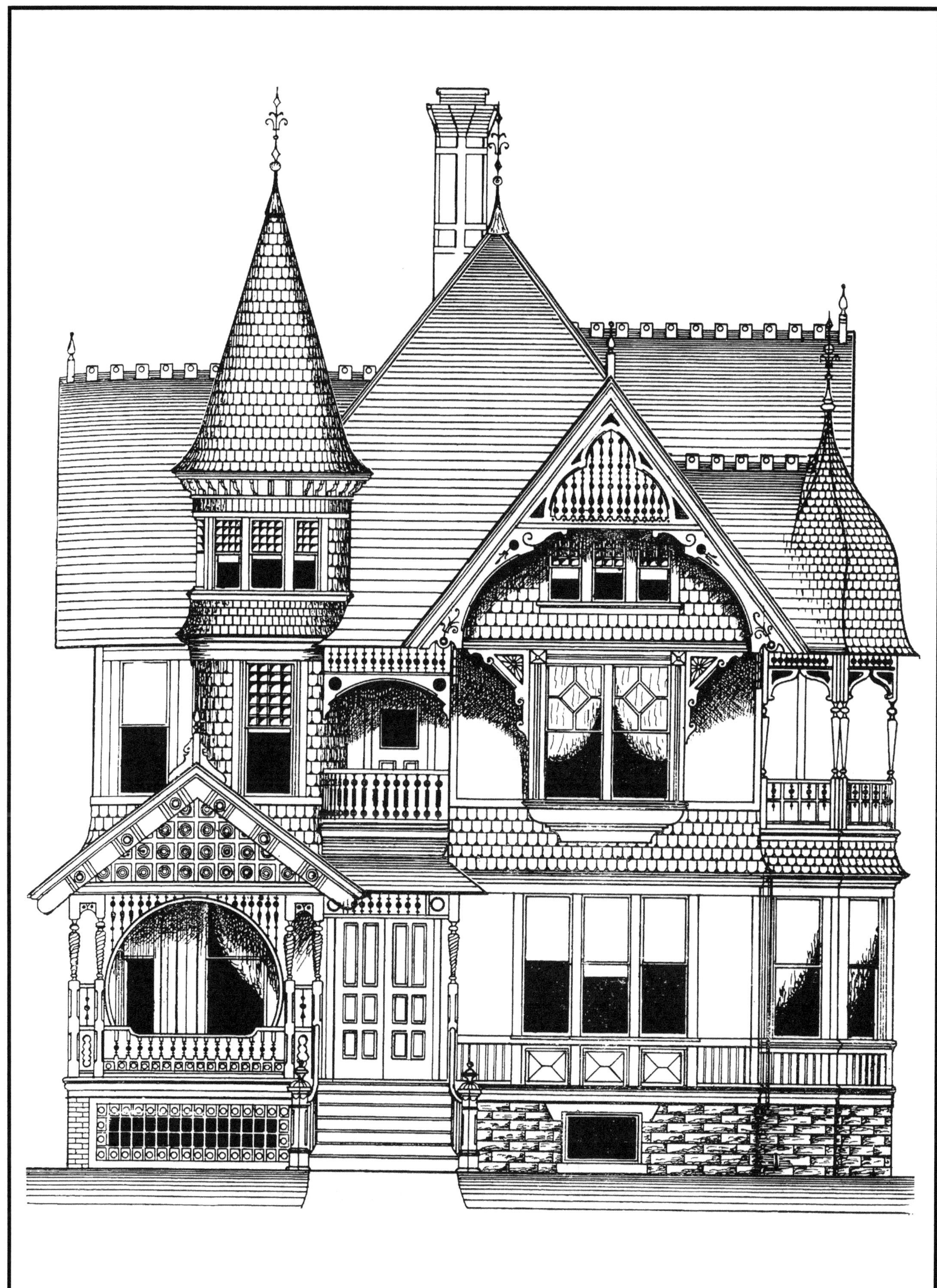

About the illustration on the reverse of this page:

From *The Cottage Souvenir No. 2* (1891)
by George F. Barber, Architect
Published by Geo. F. Barber & Co., Knoxville, Tennessee

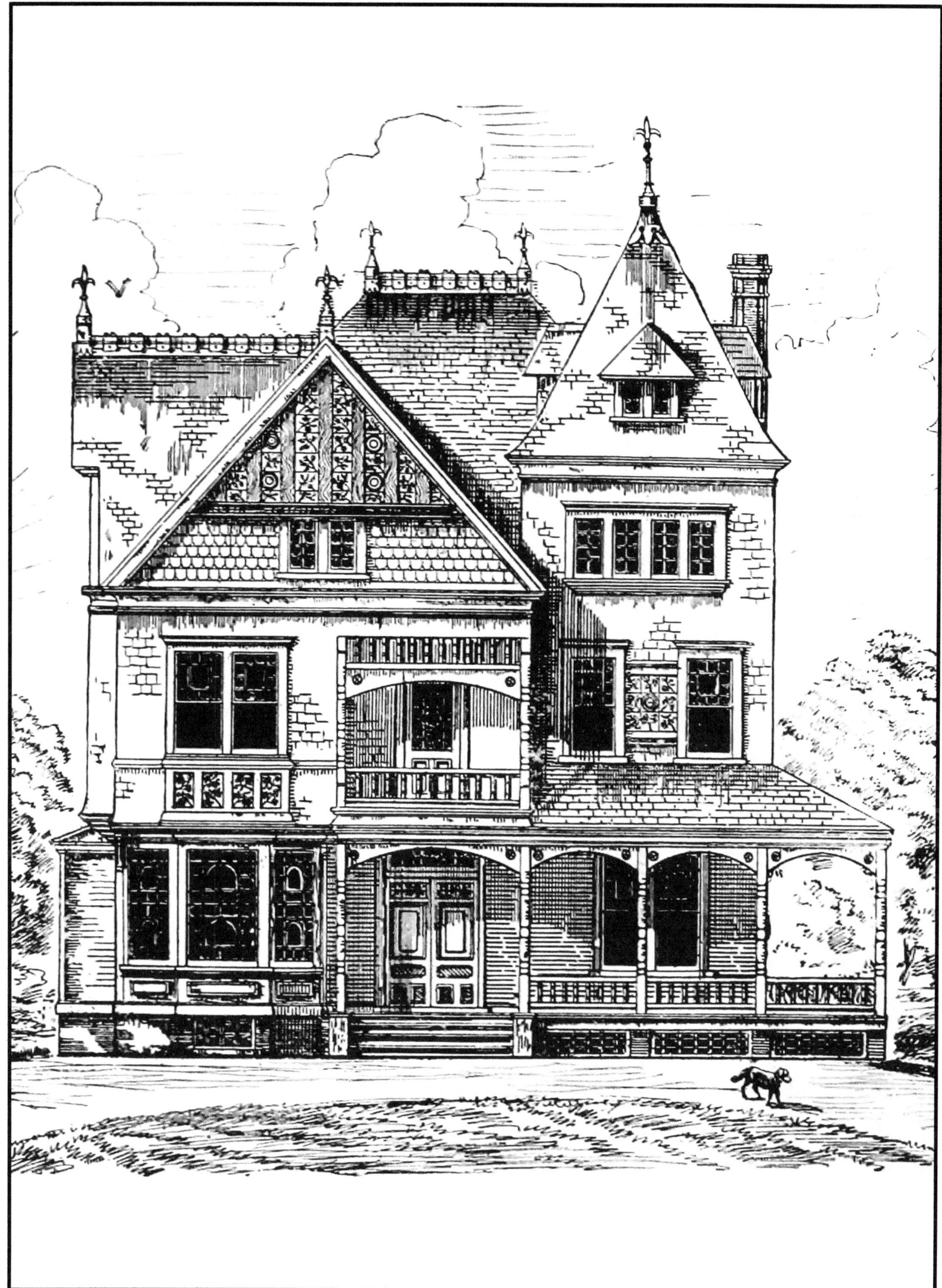

About the illustration on the reverse of this page:

From *Dwellings for Village and Country* (1885)
by Samuel Burrage Reed, Architect
Published by O. Judd Co., New York, New York

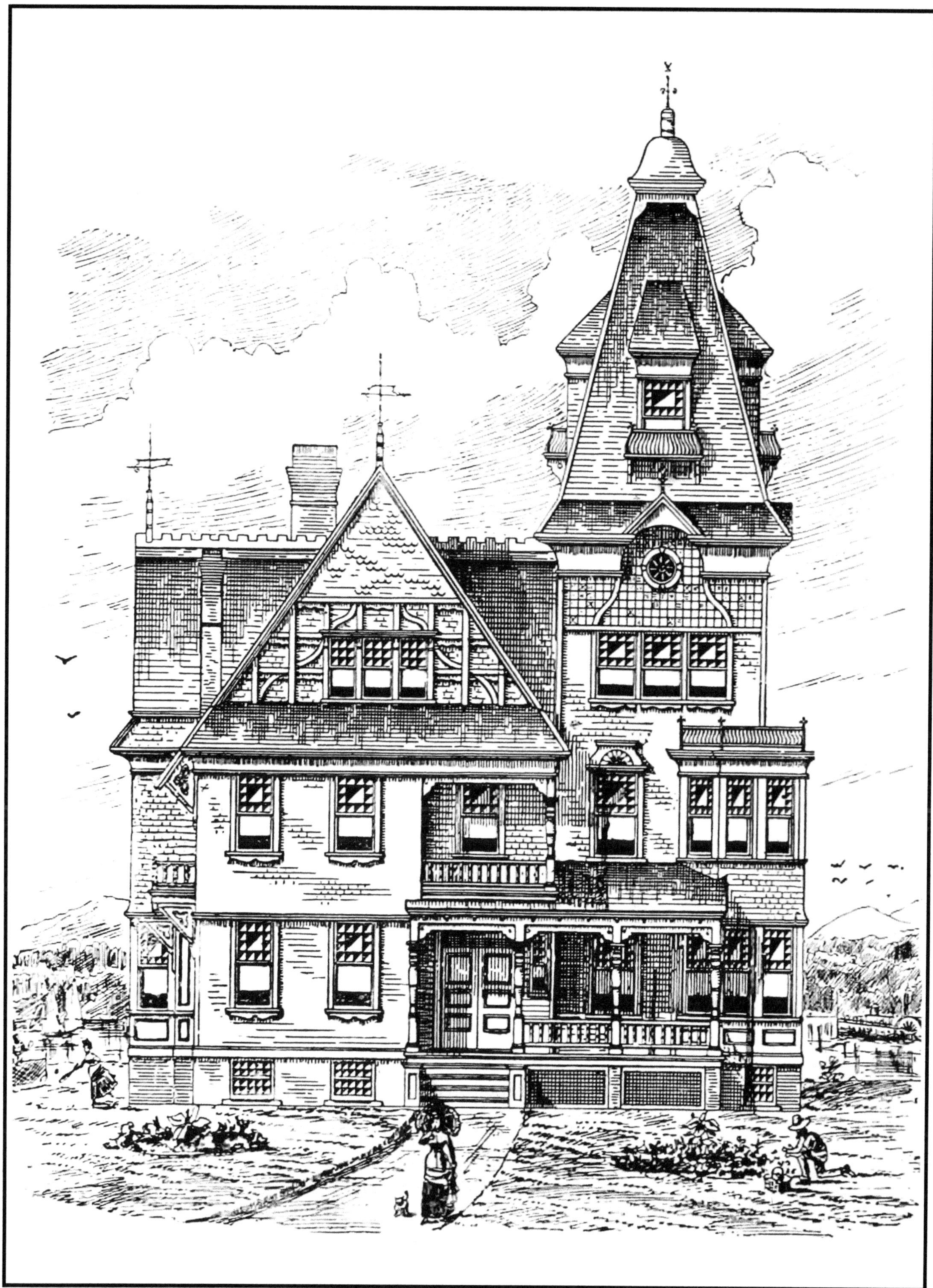

About the illustration on the reverse of this page:

From *Dwellings for Village and Country* (1885)
by Samuel Burrage Reed, Architect
Published by O. Judd Co., New York, New York

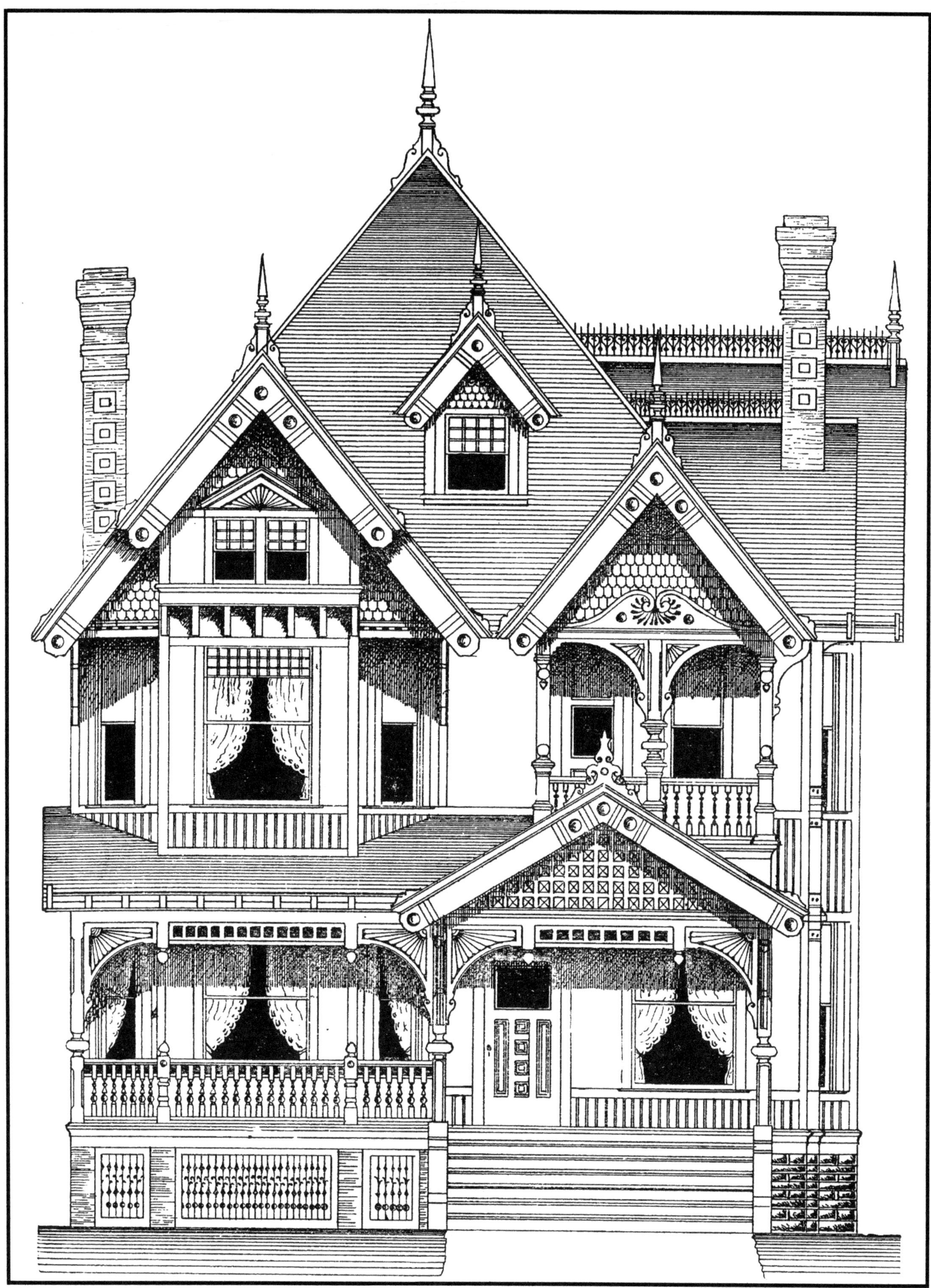

About the illustration on the reverse of this page:

From *The Cottage Souvenir No. 2* (1891)
by George F. Barber, Architect
Published by Geo. F. Barber & Co., Knoxville, Tennessee

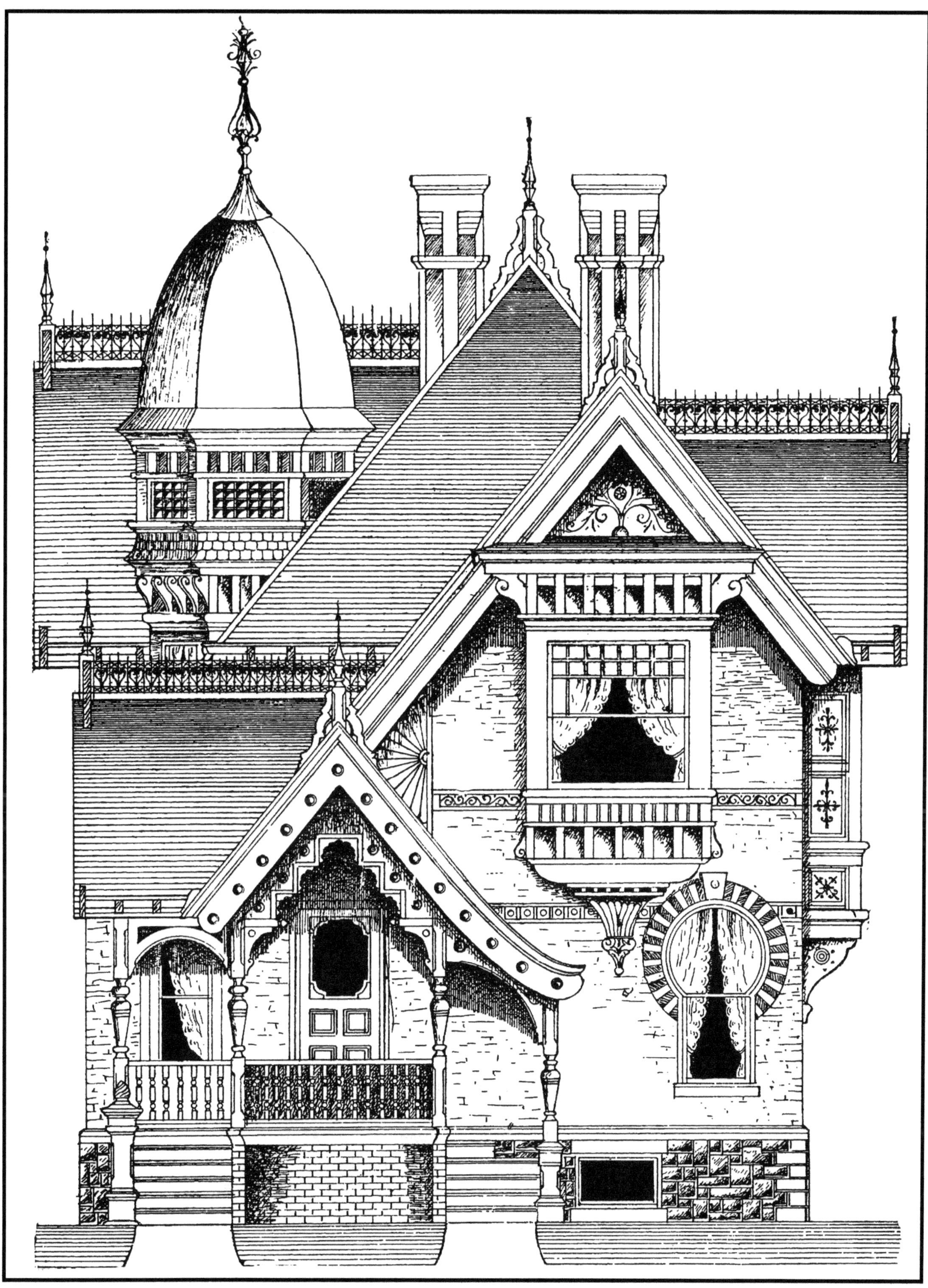

About the illustration on the reverse of this page:

From *The Cottage Souvenir No. 2* (1891)
by George F. Barber, Architect
Published by Geo. F. Barber & Co., Knoxville, Tennessee

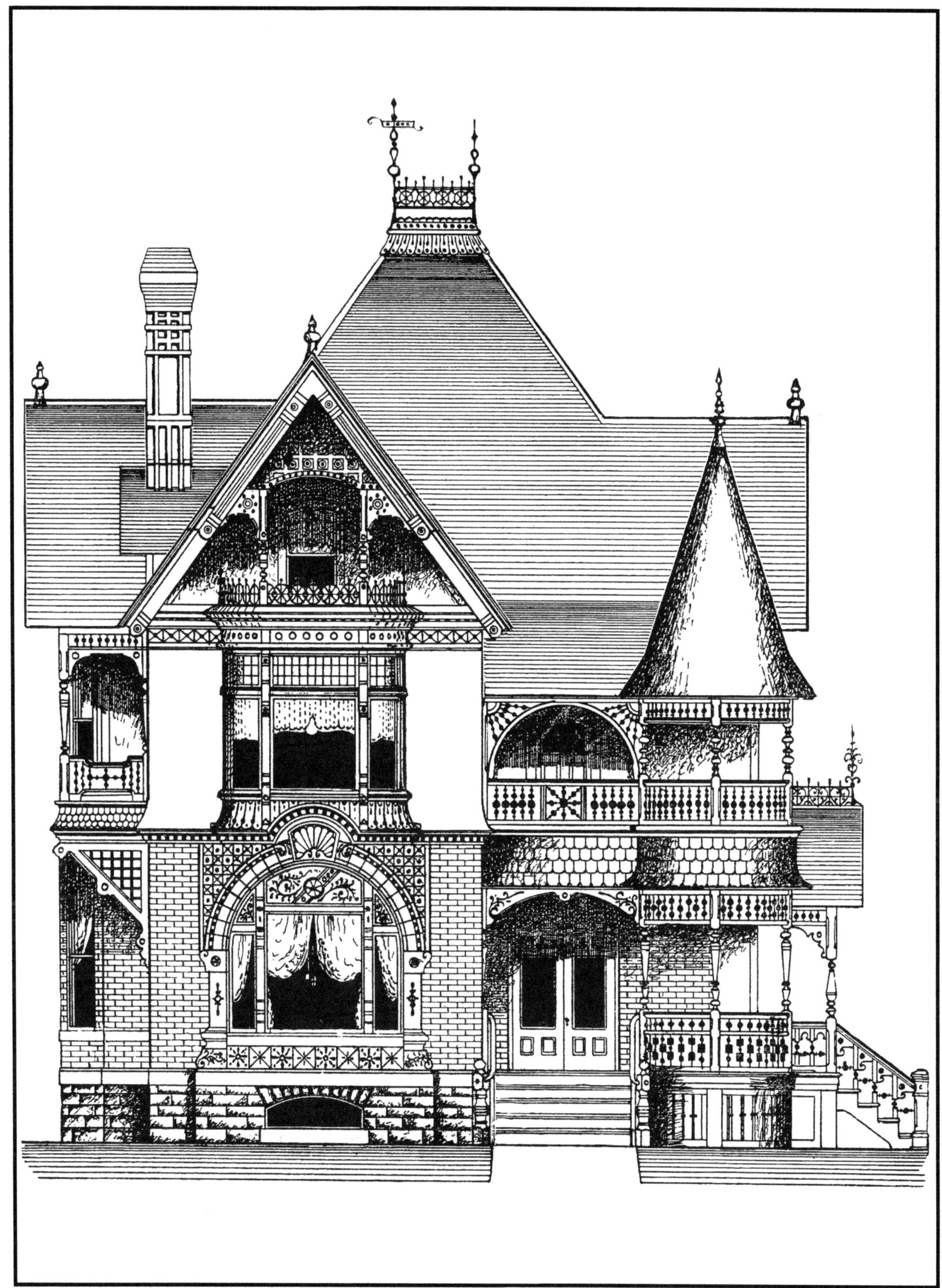

About the illustration on the reverse of this page:

From *The Cottage Souvenir Fourth Edition, Revised* (1896)
by George F. Barber, Architect
Published by Geo. F. Barber & Co., Knoxville, Tennessee

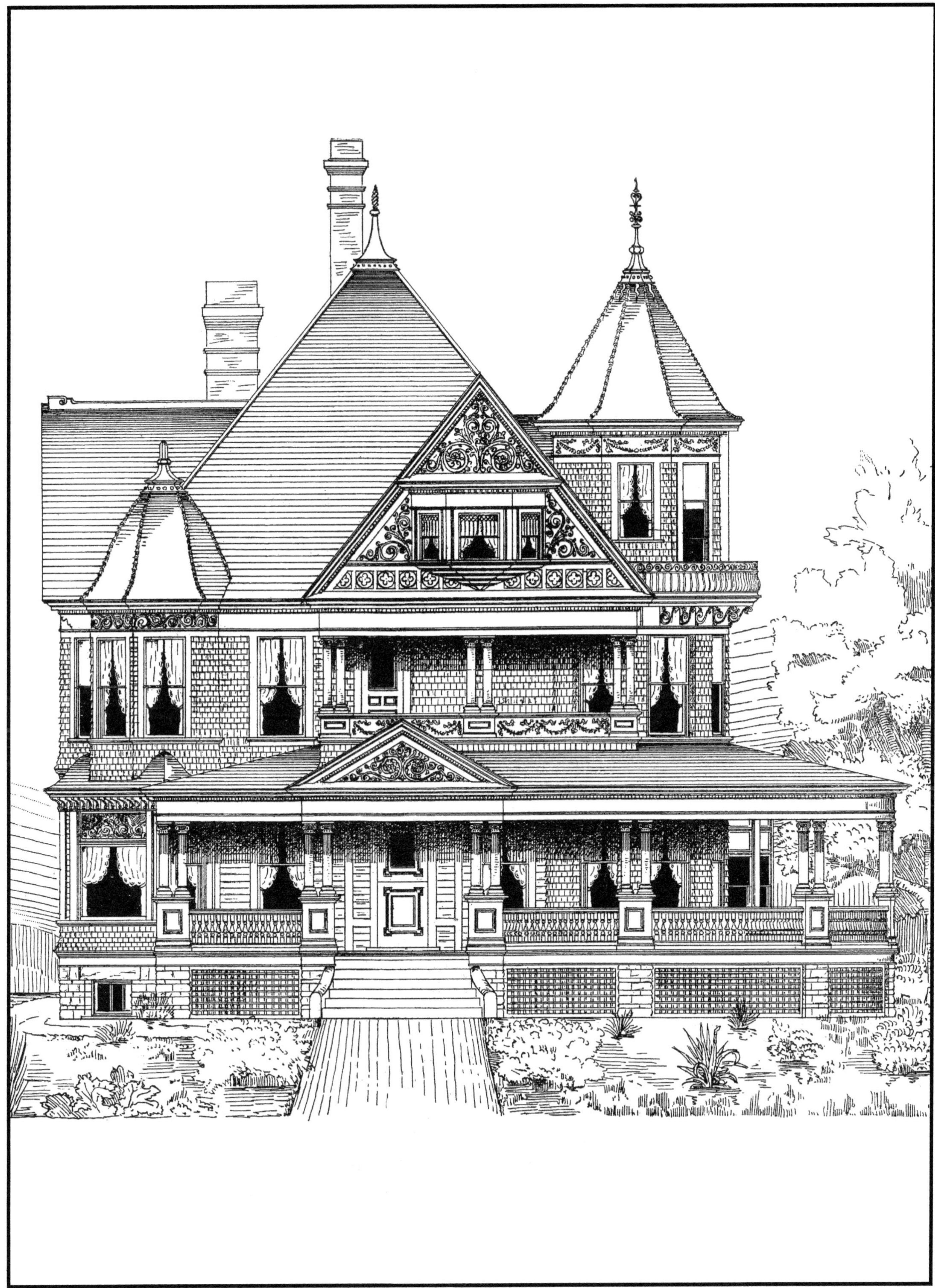

About the illustration on the reverse of this page:

From *The Cottage Souvenir Fourth Edition, Revised* (1896)
by George F. Barber, Architect
Published by Geo. F. Barber & Co., Knoxville, Tennessee

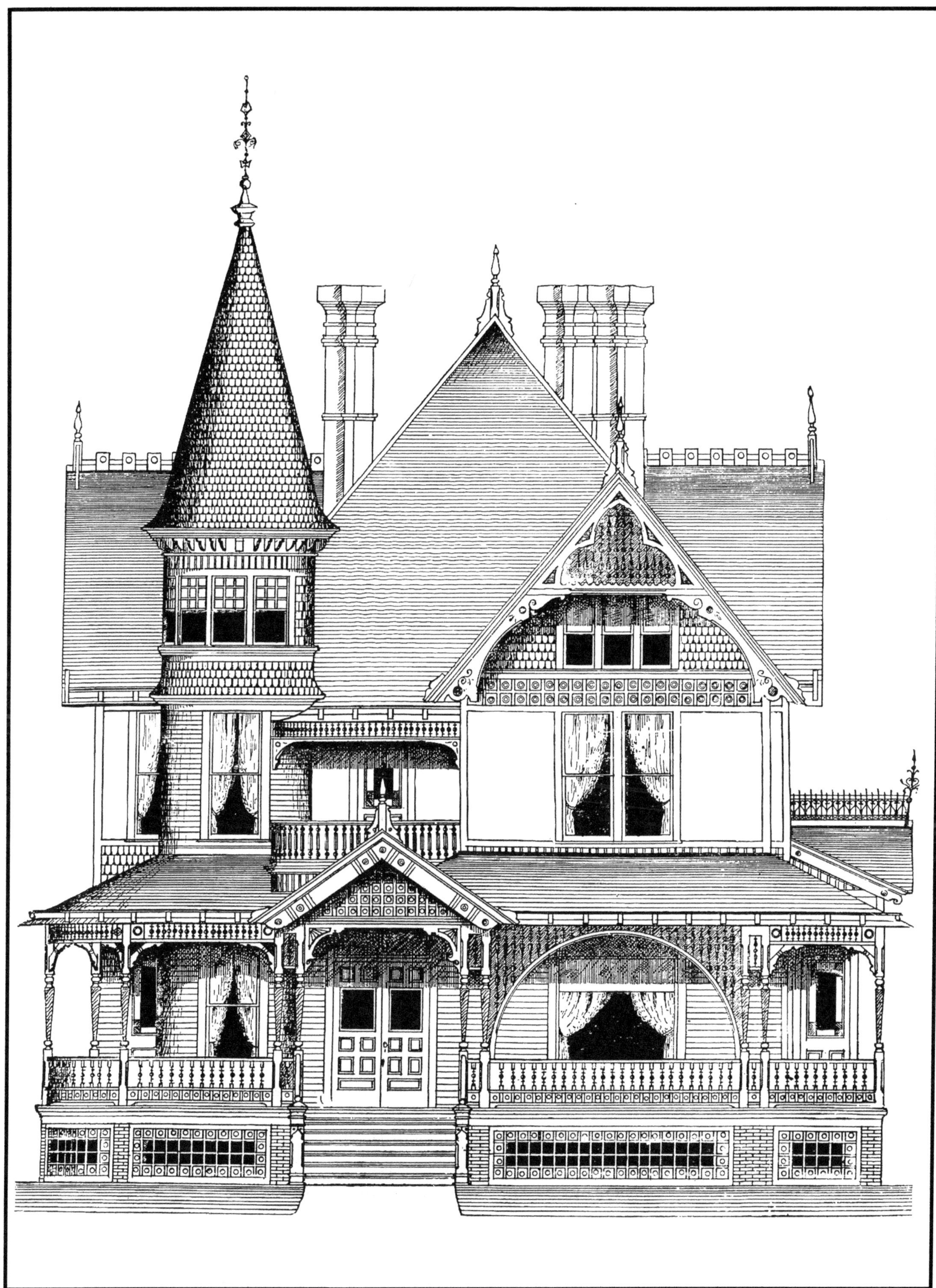

About the illustration on the reverse of this page:

From *The Cottage Souvenir No. 2* (1891)
by George F. Barber, Architect
Published by Geo. F. Barber & Co., Knoxville, Tennessee

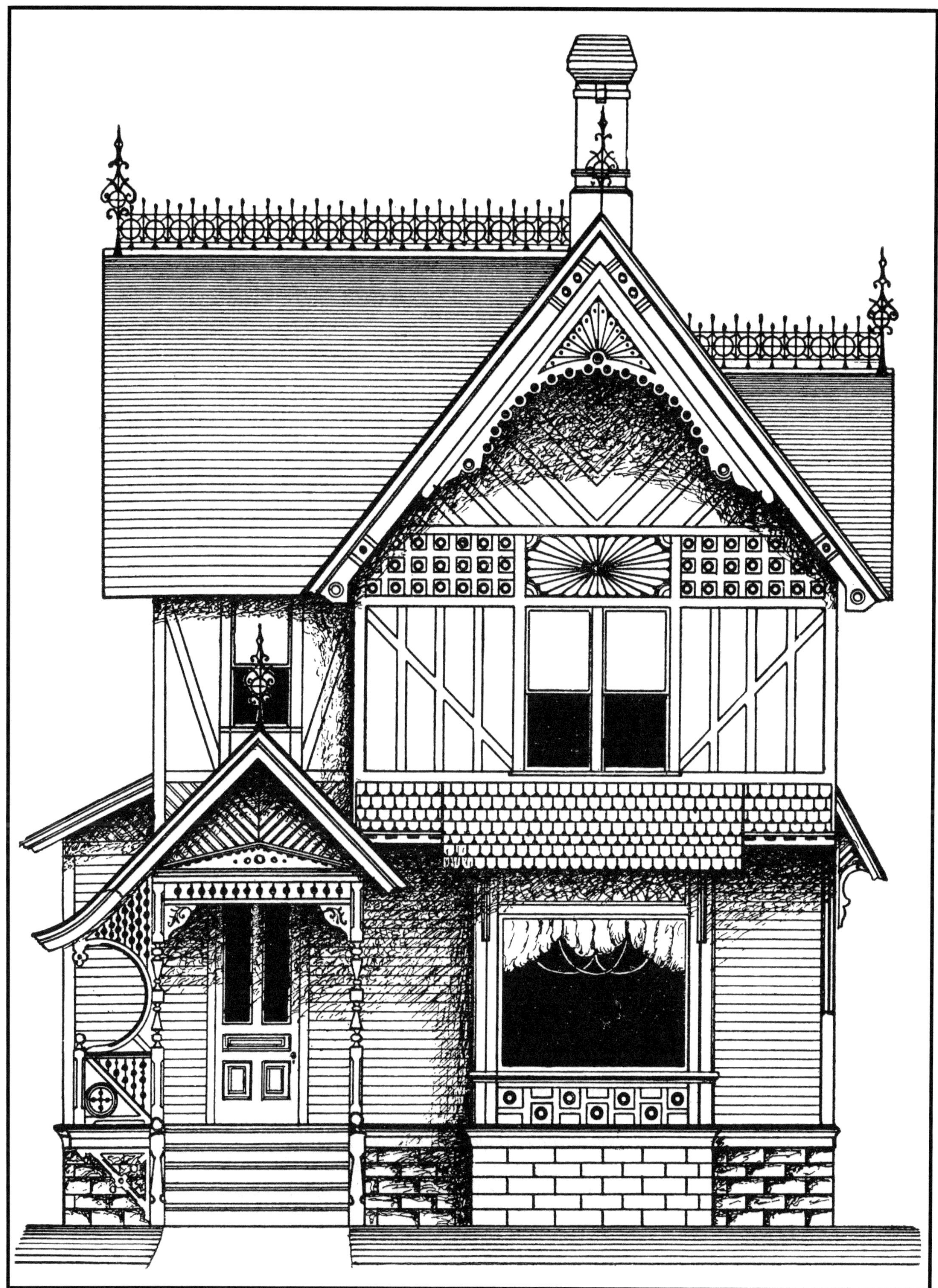

About the illustration on the reverse of this page:

From *The Cottage Souvenir No. 2* (1891)
by George F. Barber, Architect
Published by Geo. F. Barber & Co., Knoxville, Tennessee

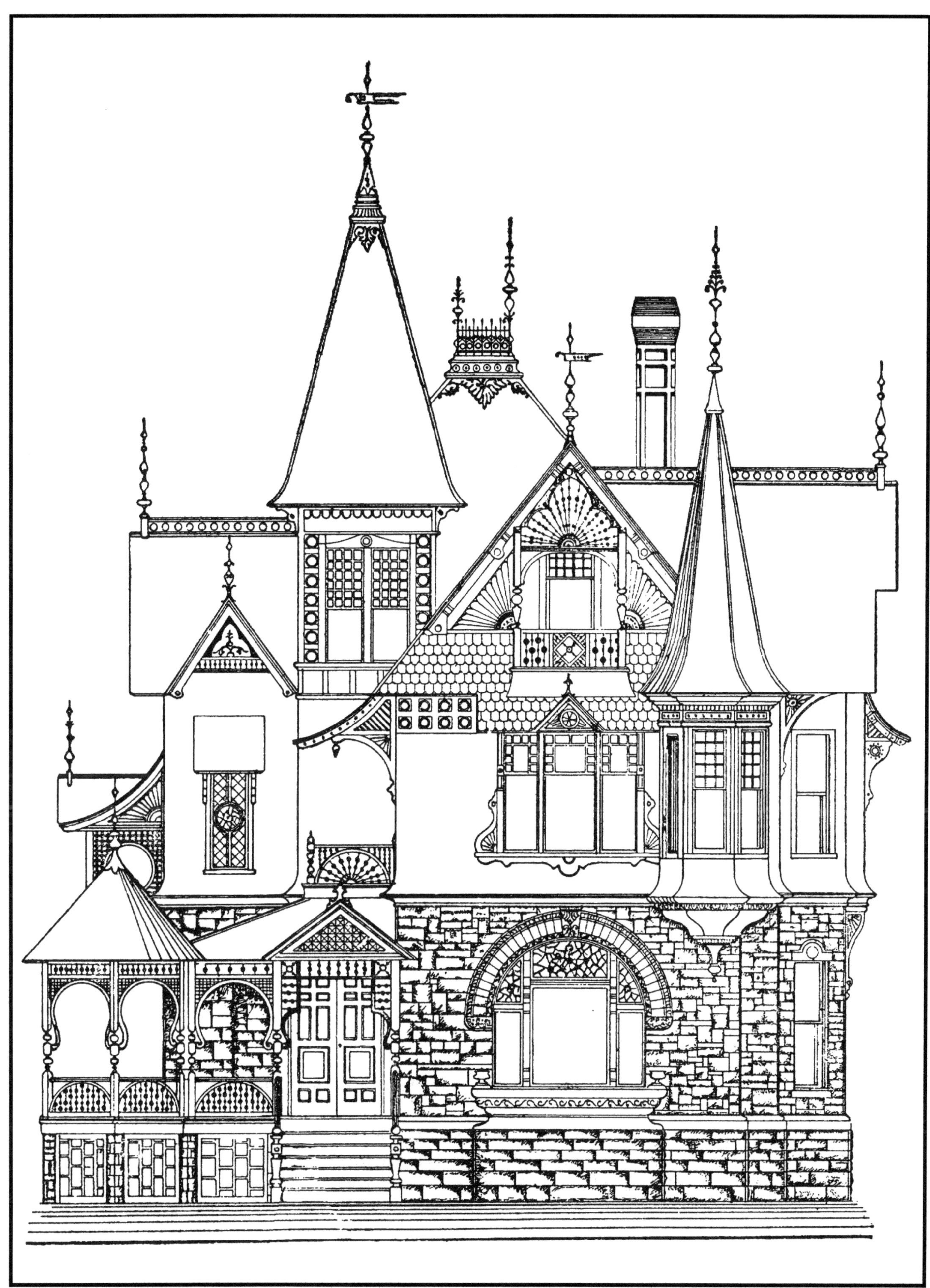

About the illustration on the reverse of this page:

From *The Cottage Souvenir No. 2* (1891)
by George F. Barber, Architect
Published by Geo. F. Barber & Co., Knoxville, Tennessee

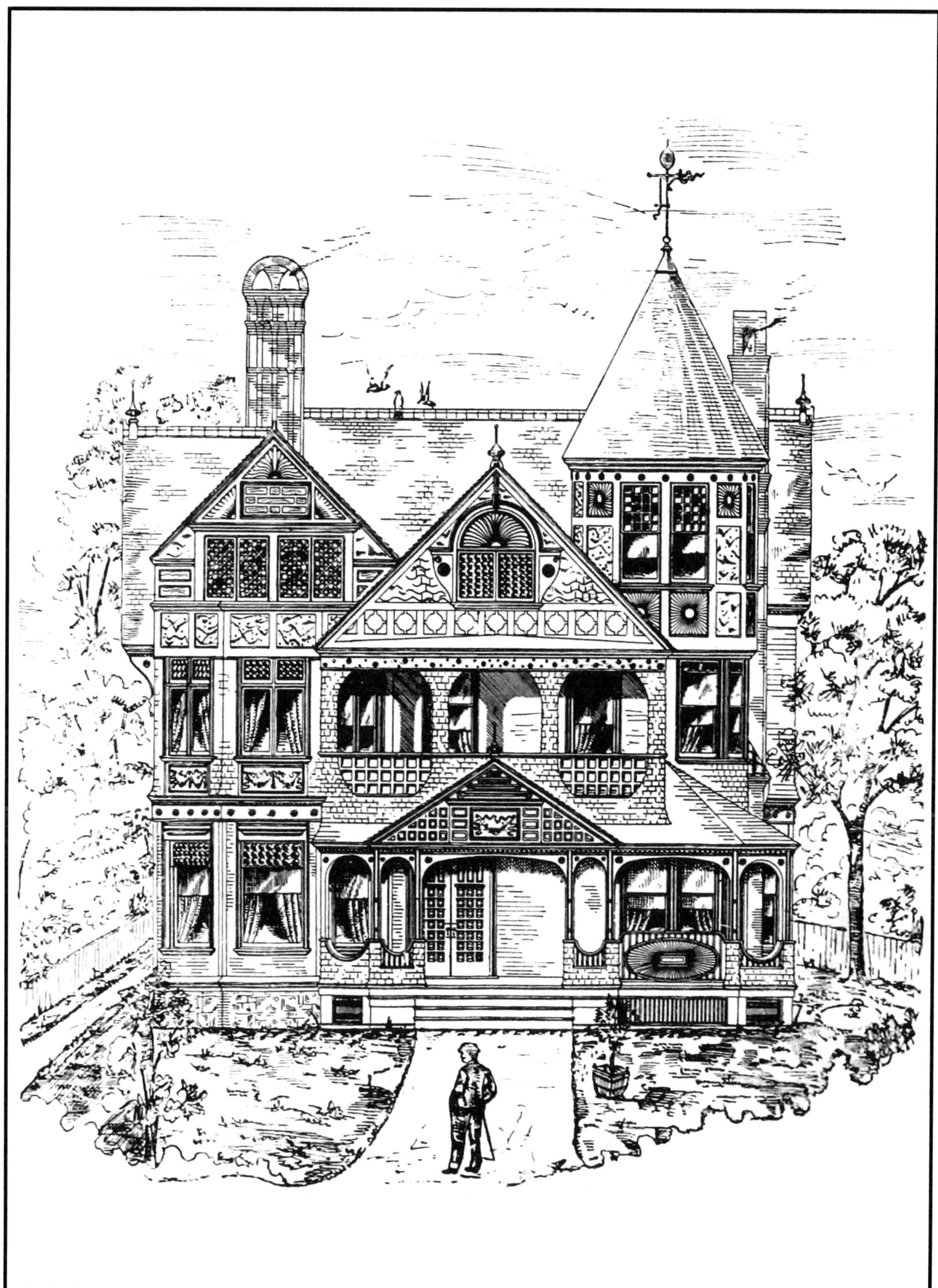

About the illustration on the reverse of this page:

From *Dwellings for Village and Country* (1885)
by Samuel Burrage Reed, Architect
Published by O. Judd Co., New York, New York

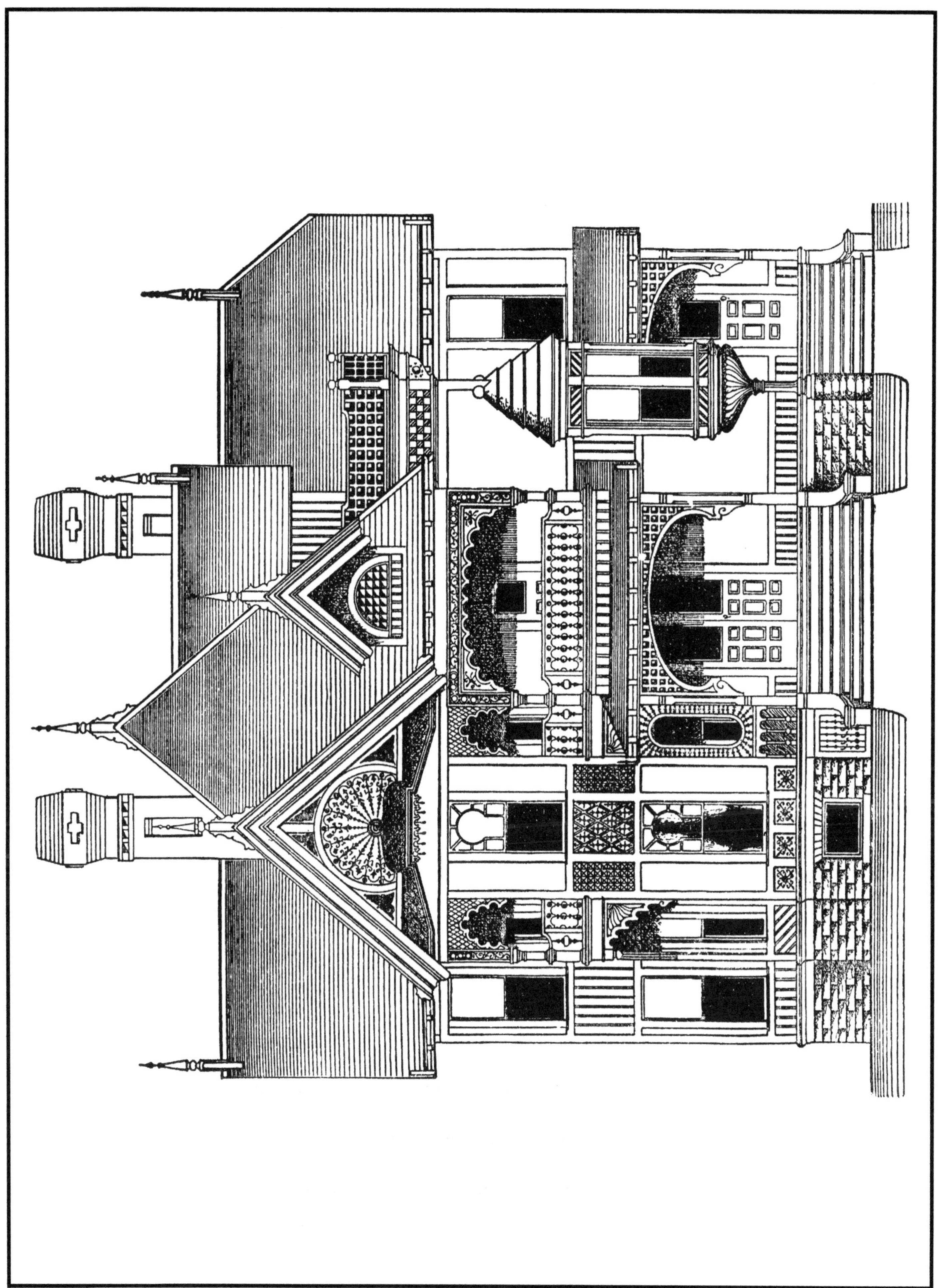

About the illustration on the reverse of this page:

From *The Cottage Souvenir No. 2* (1891)
by George F. Barber, Architect
Published by Geo. F. Barber & Co., Knoxville, Tennessee

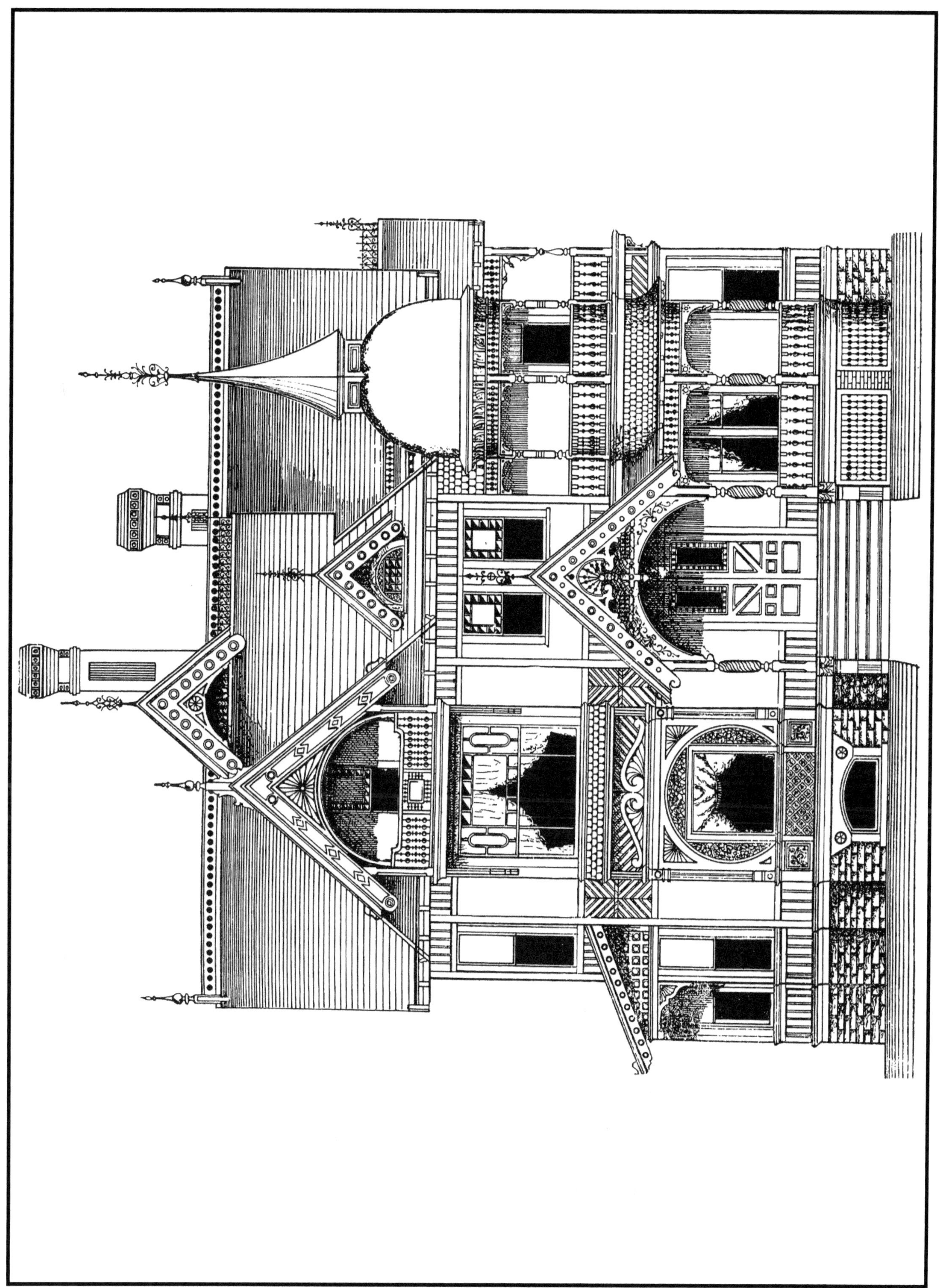

About the illustration on the reverse of this page:

From *The Cottage Souvenir No. 2* (1891)
by George F. Barber, Architect
Published by Geo. F. Barber & Co., Knoxville, Tennessee

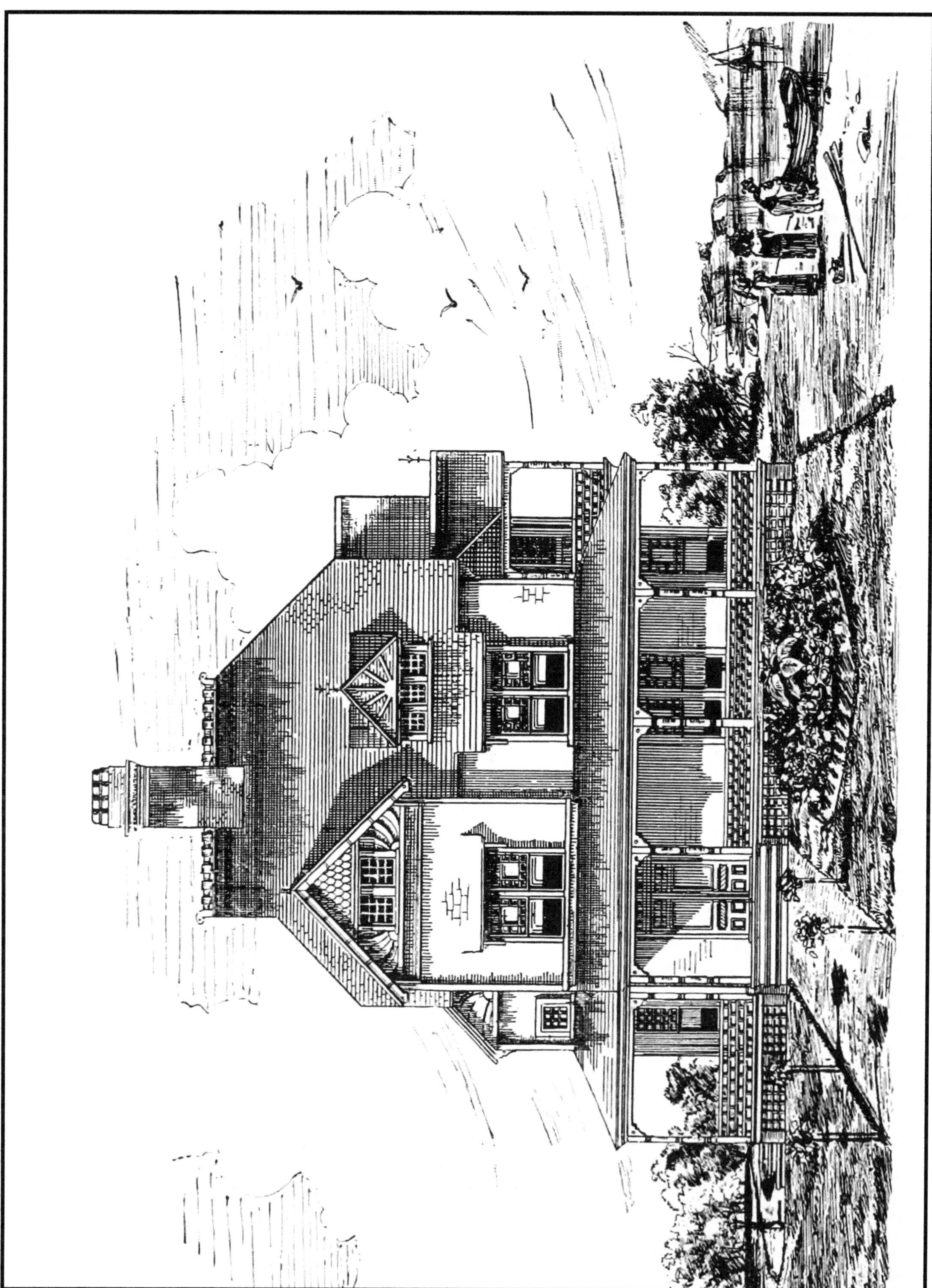

About the illustration on the reverse of this page:

From *Dwellings for Village and Country* (1885)
by Samuel Burrage Reed, Architect
Published by O. Judd Co., New York, New York

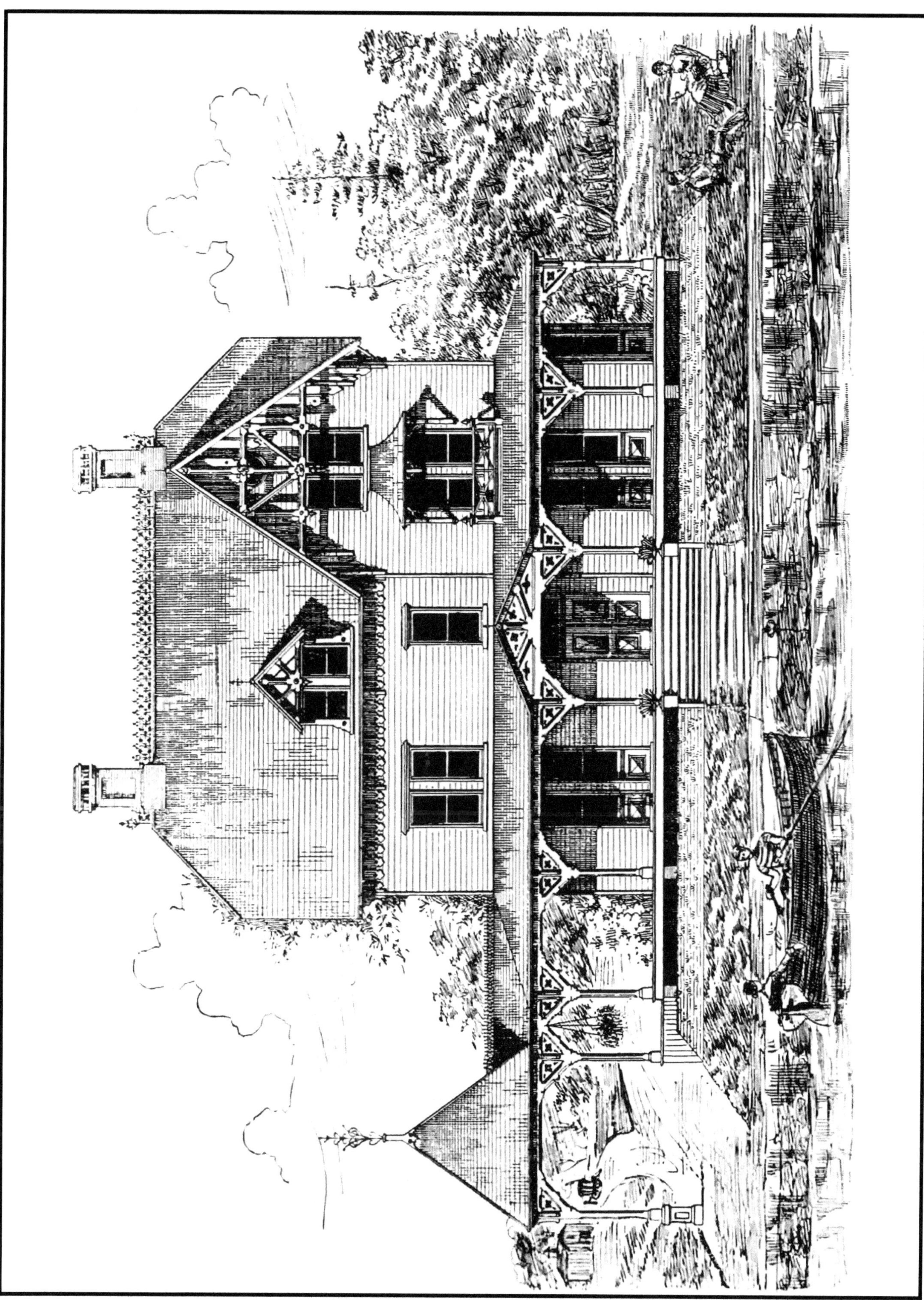

About the illustration on the reverse of this page:

From *Dwellings for Village and Country* (1885)
by Samuel Burrage Reed, Architect
Published by O. Judd Co., New York, New York

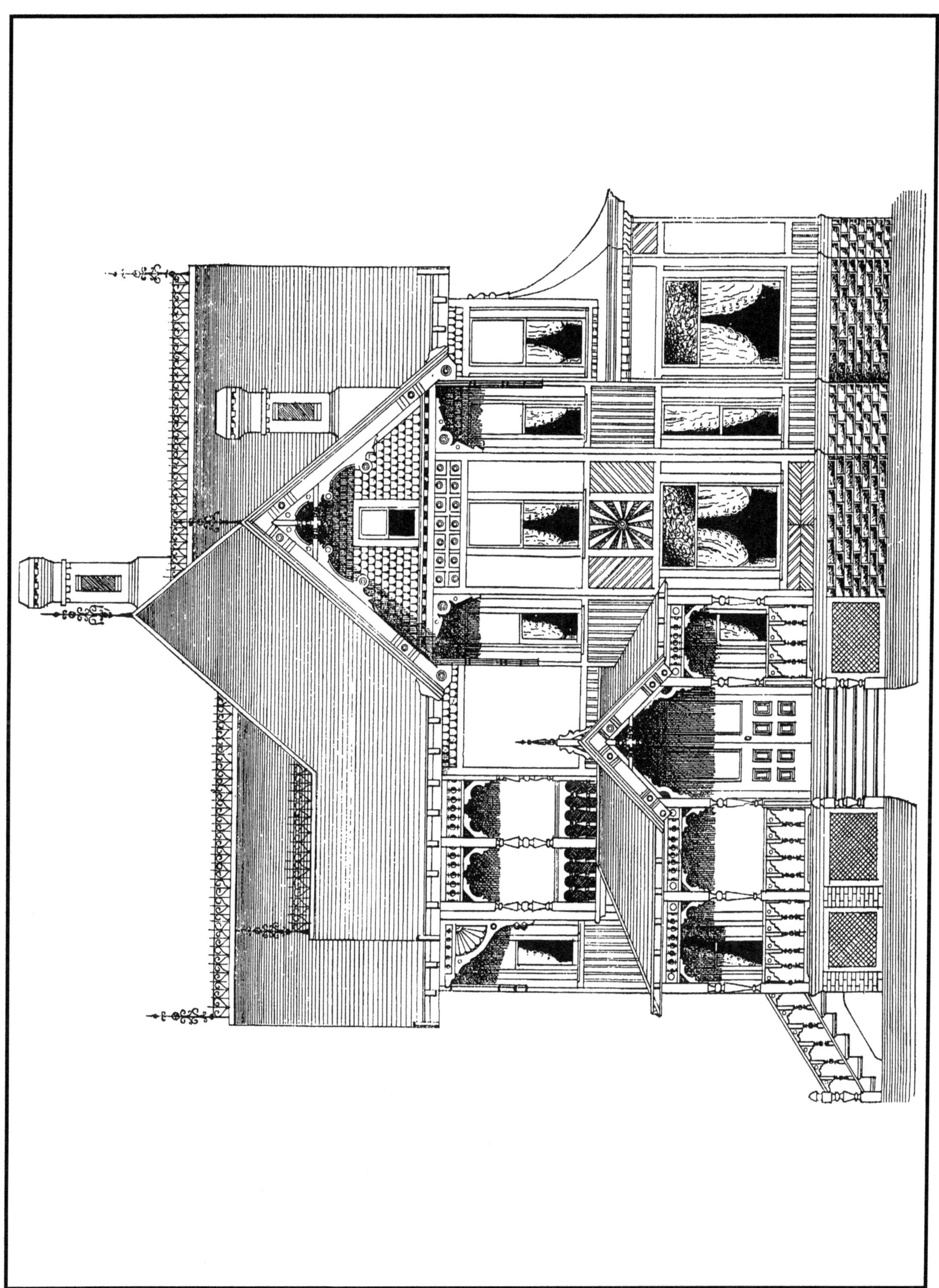

About the illustration on the reverse of this page:

From *The Cottage Souvenir No. 2* (1891)
by George F. Barber, Architect
Published by Geo. F. Barber & Co., Knoxville, Tennessee

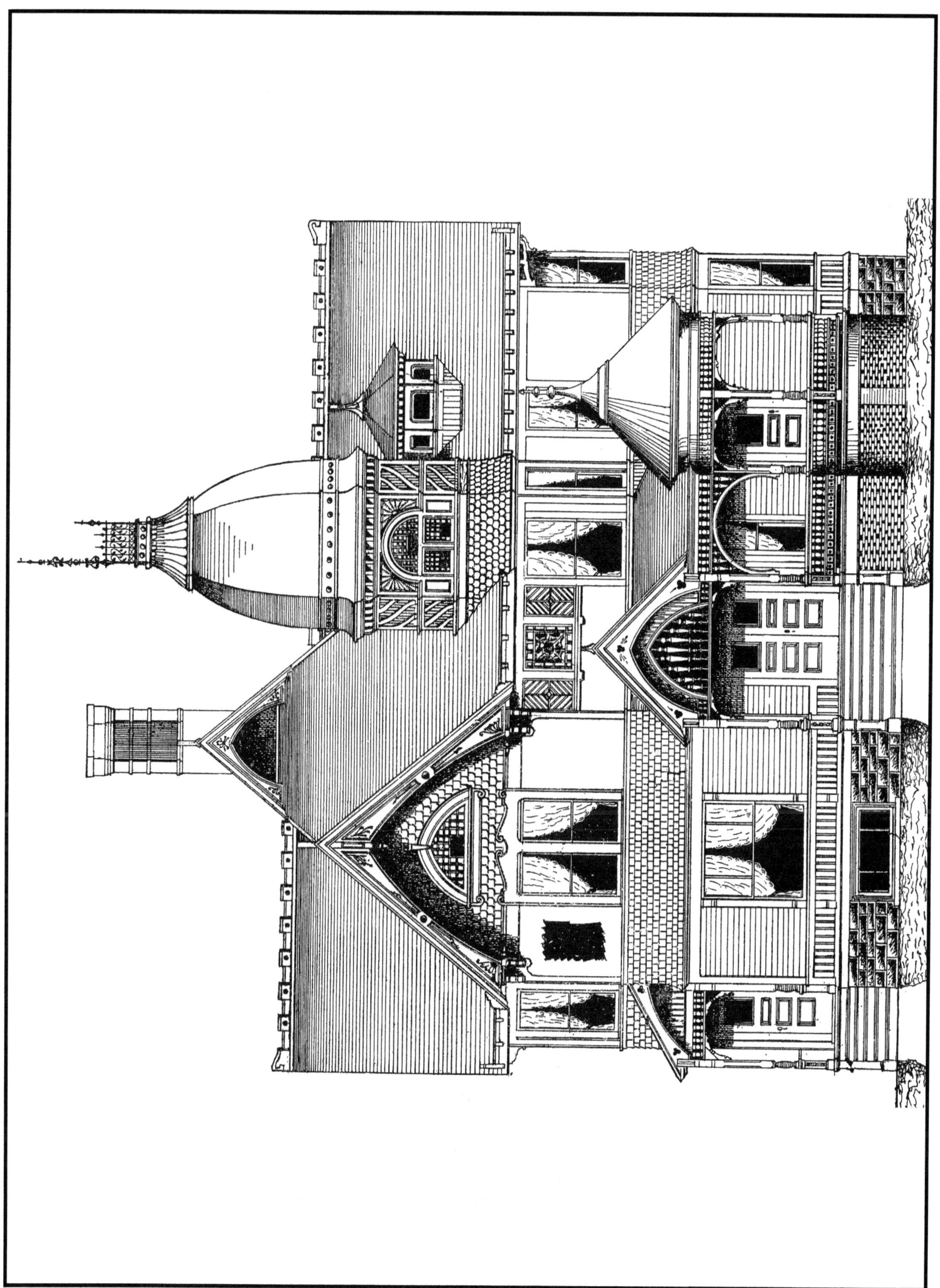

About the illustration on the reverse of this page:

From *The Cottage Souvenir Fourth Edition, Revised* (1896)
by George F. Barber, Architect
Published by Geo. F. Barber & Co., Knoxville, Tennessee

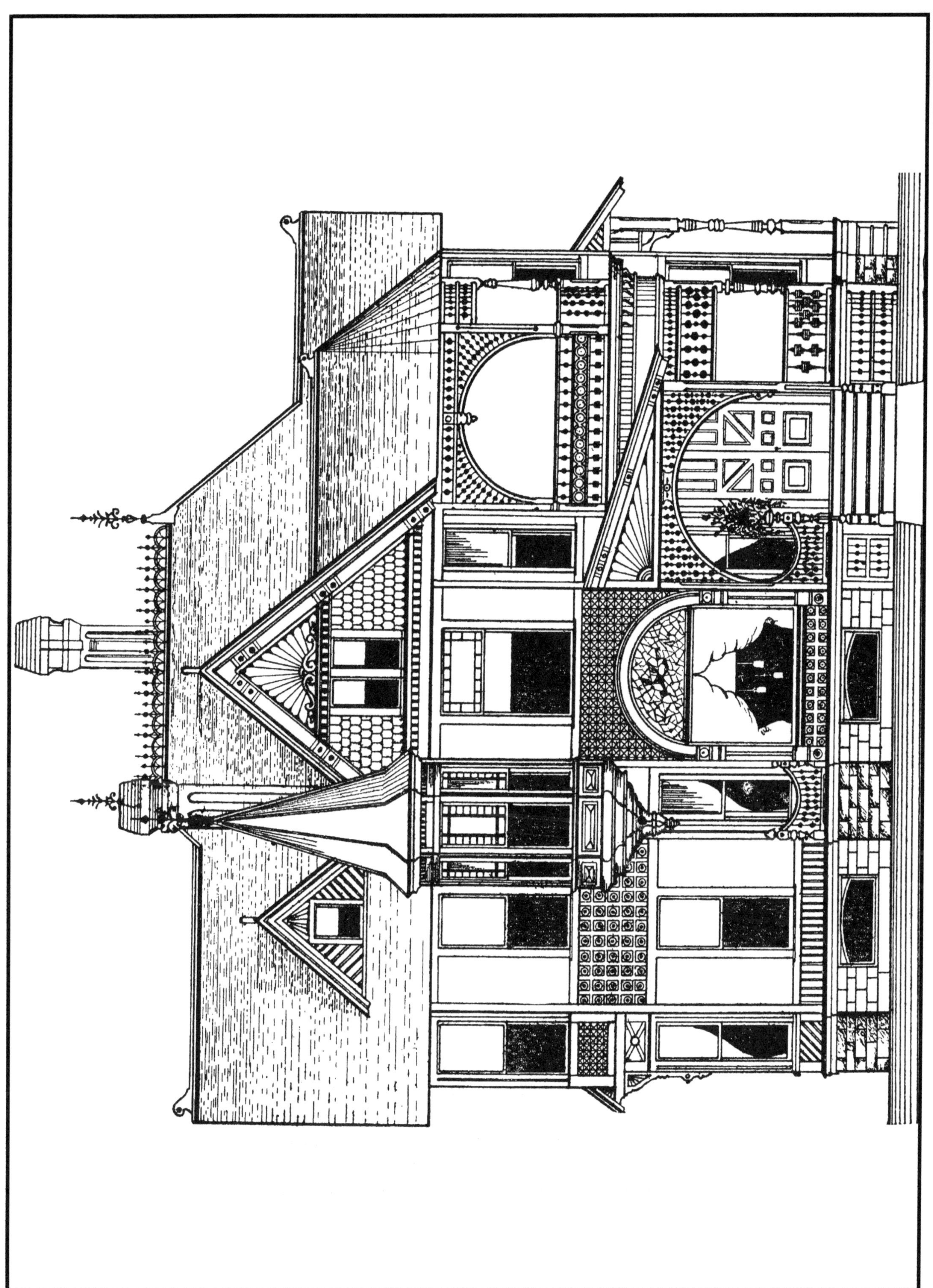

About the illustration on the reverse of this page:

From *The Cottage Souvenir No. 2* (1891)
by George F. Barber, Architect
Published by Geo. F. Barber & Co., Knoxville, Tennessee

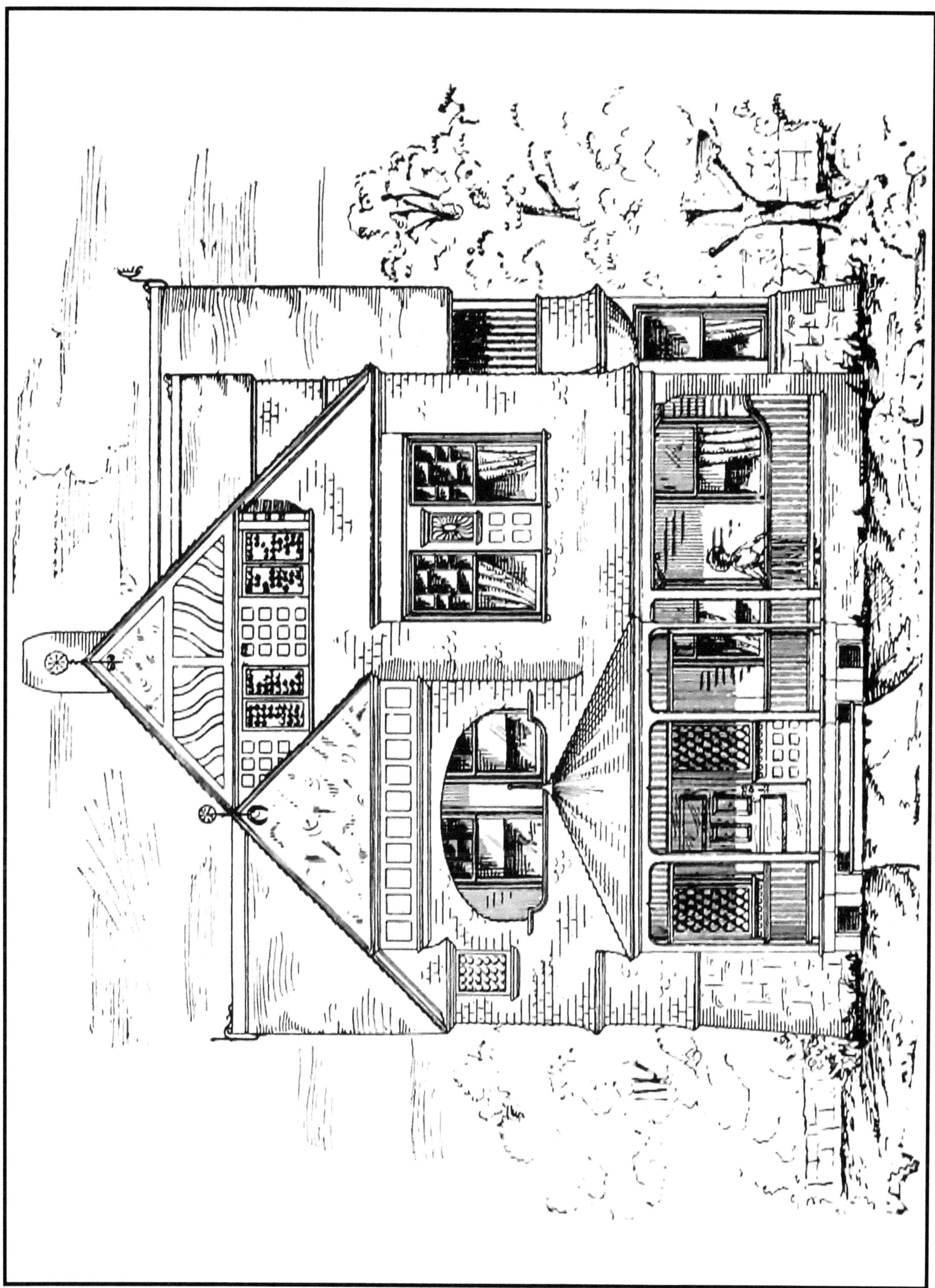

About the illustration on the reverse of this page:

From *Dwellings for Village and Country* (1885)
by Samuel Burrage Reed, Architect
Published by O. Judd Co., New York, New York

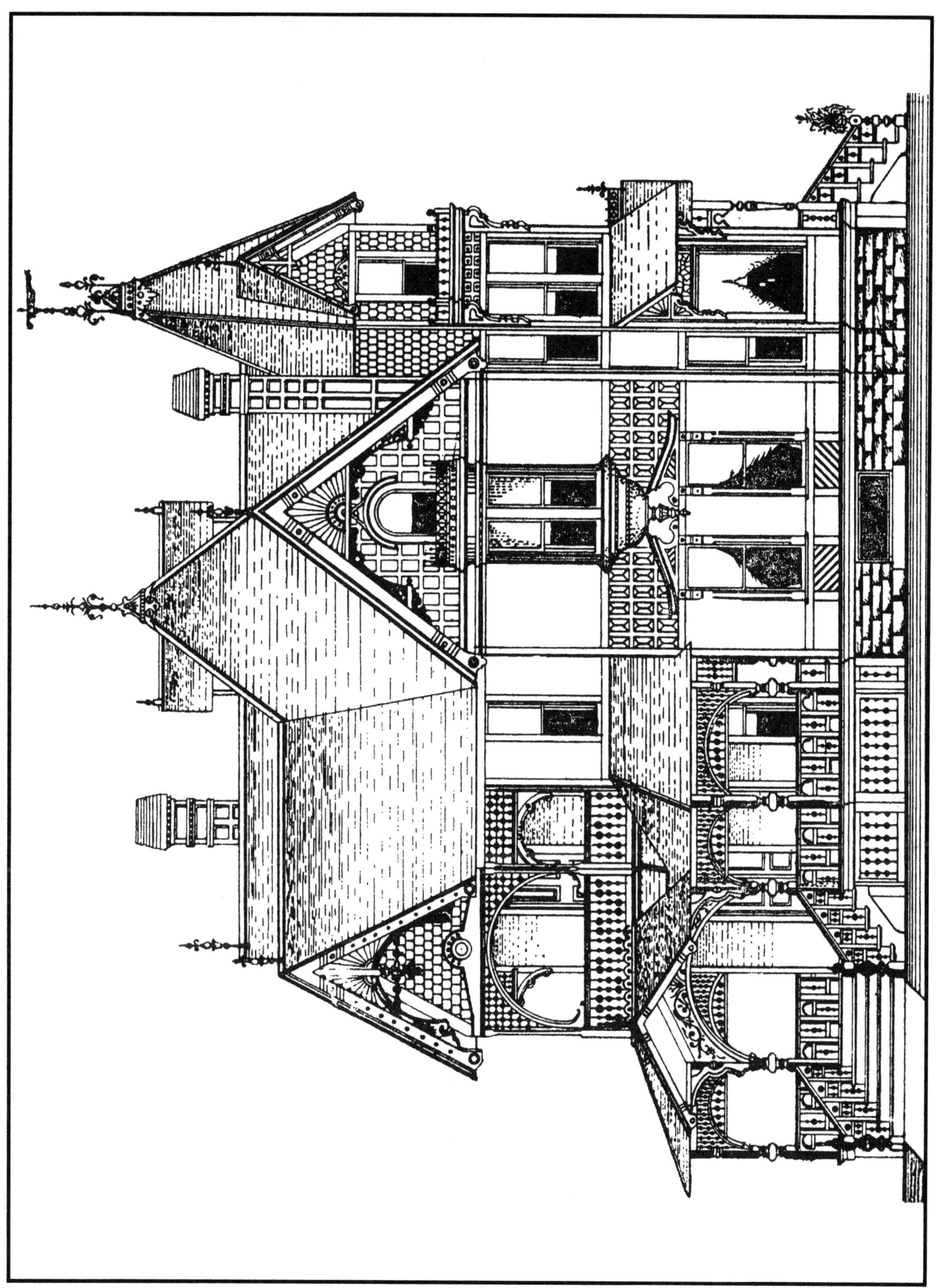

About the illustration on the reverse of this page:

From *The Cottage Souvenir No. 2* (1891)
by George F. Barber, Architect
Published by Geo. F. Barber & Co., Knoxville, Tennessee

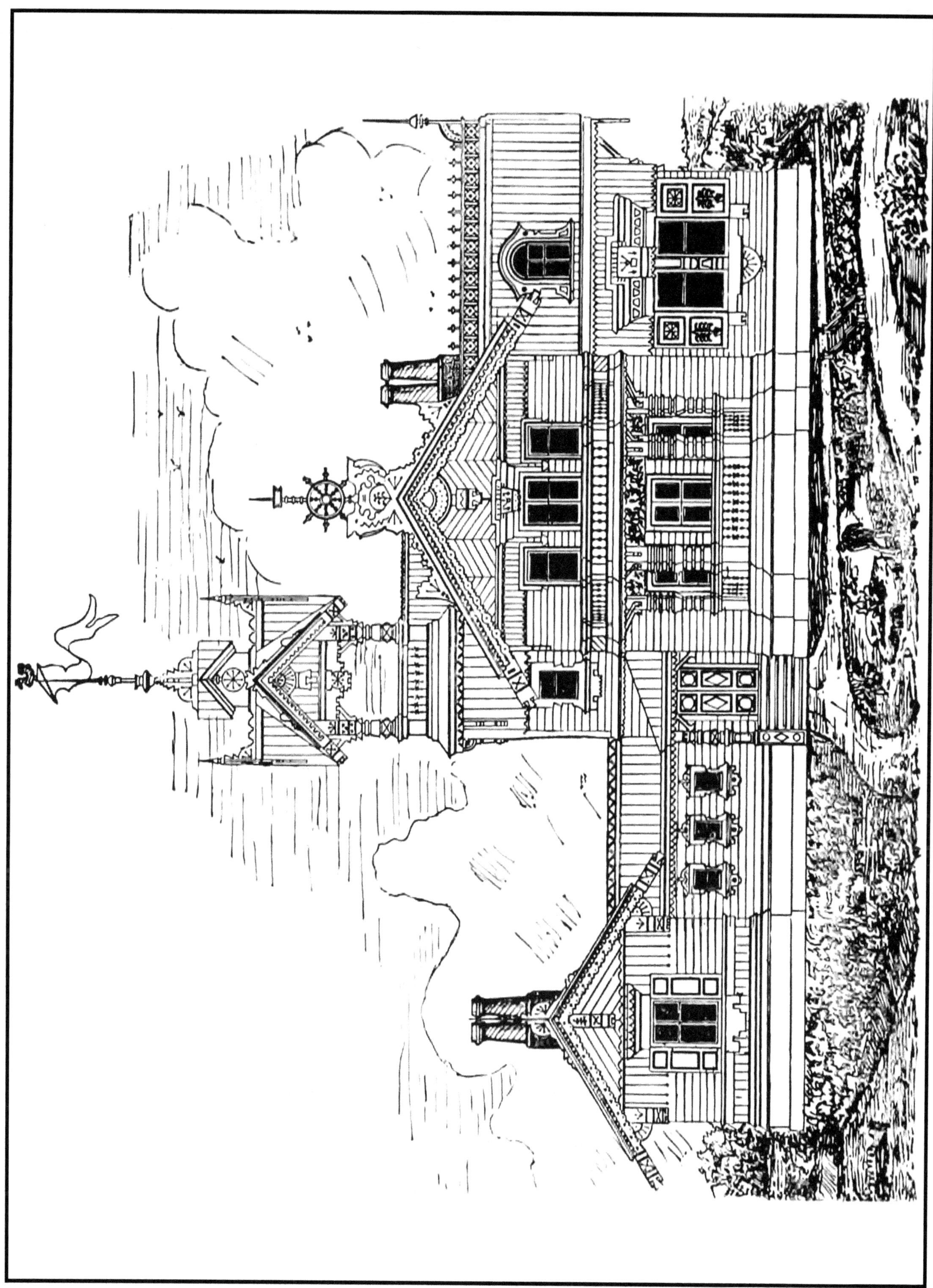

About the illustration on the reverse of this page:

From *Dwellings for Village and Country* (1885)
by Samuel Burrage Reed, Architect
Published by O. Judd Co., New York, New York

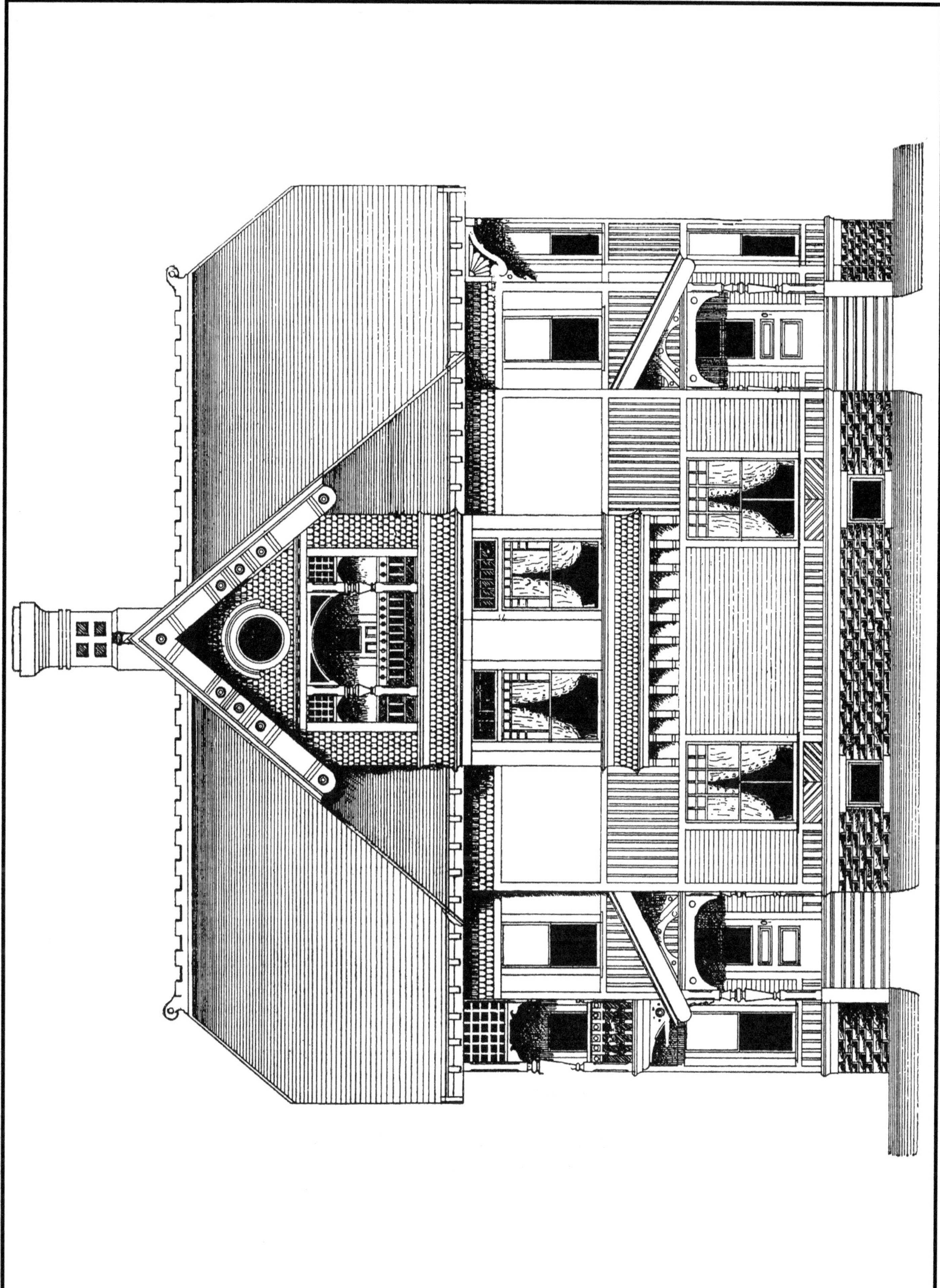

About the illustration on the reverse of this page:

From *The Cottage Souvenir No. 2* (1891)
by George F. Barber, Architect
Published by Geo. F. Barber & Co., Knoxville, Tennessee

THE END

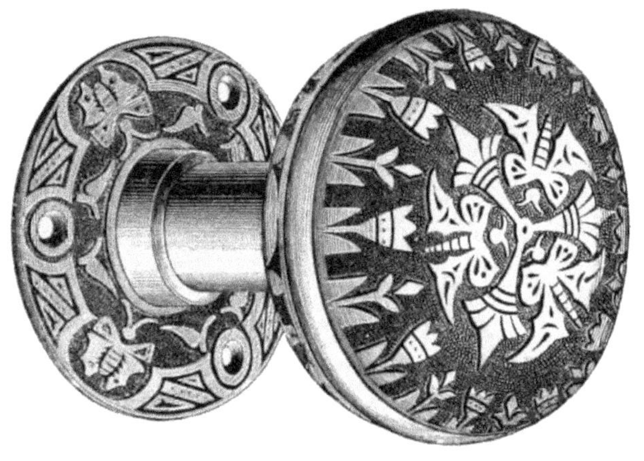

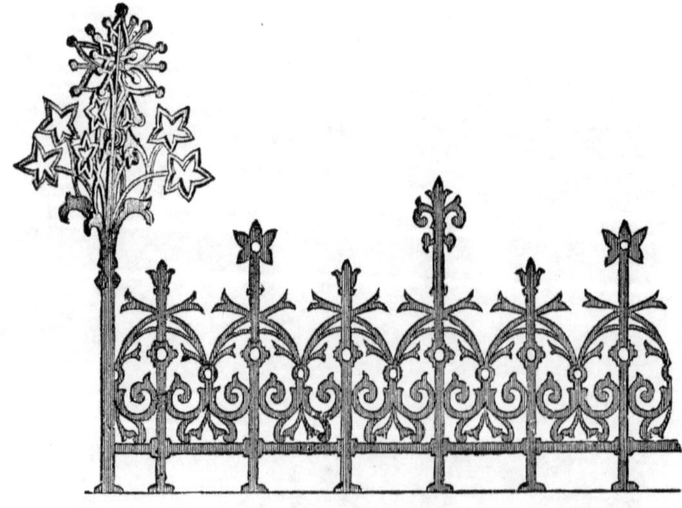

BONUS! FREE BOOKMARKS

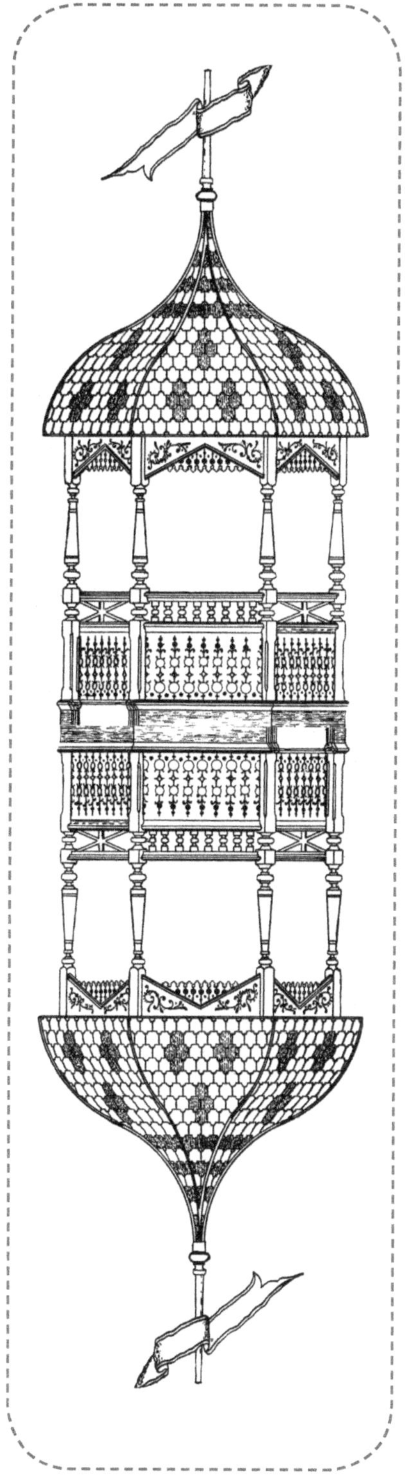

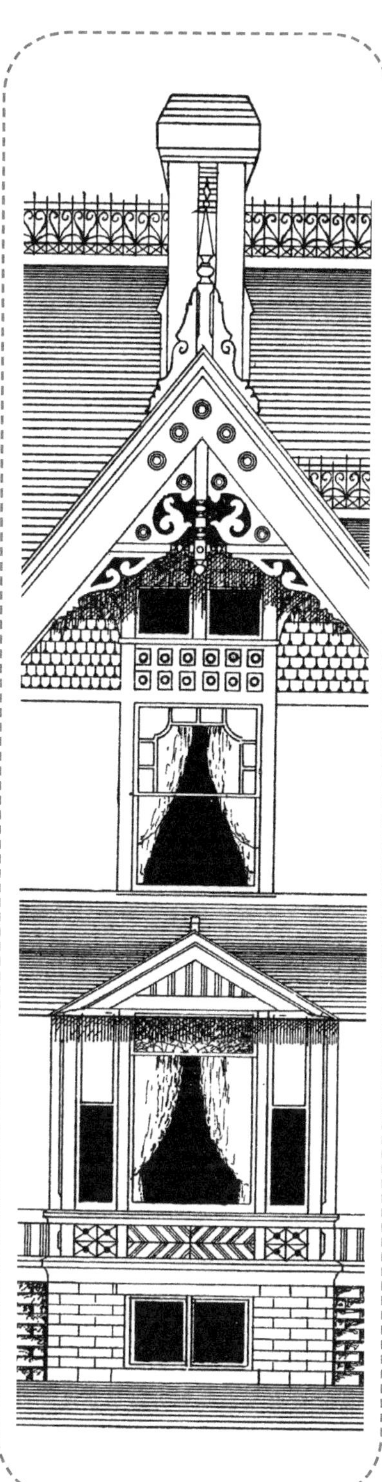

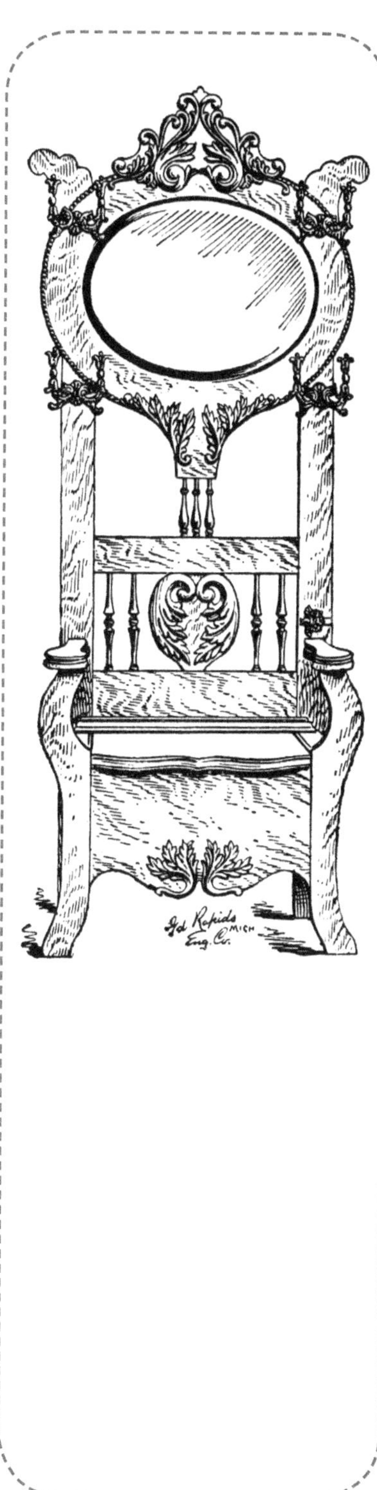

After coloring the images, you can (1) Paste the bookmark on a thick piece of paper and cut it out on the dotted lines, or (2) Cut it out on the dotted lines and laminate each bookmark.

LIKE THIS BOOK? WE HAVE OTHERS!

For more coloring, look for our *Vintage Women: Adult Coloring Book* series

Also from Synchronista...
The Beer Lover's Guide to Vintage Advertising
Something Old: Vintage Wedding Dress Fashion Look Book
Color on Black Adult Coloring Book: Mandalas
Motivation & Mandalas Adult Coloring Book: Inspiration for Women
Book of Brilliant Things Activity Book
Large Print Word Search Puzzles series
All-In-One Pregnancy Calendar, Daily Countdown, Planner & Journal

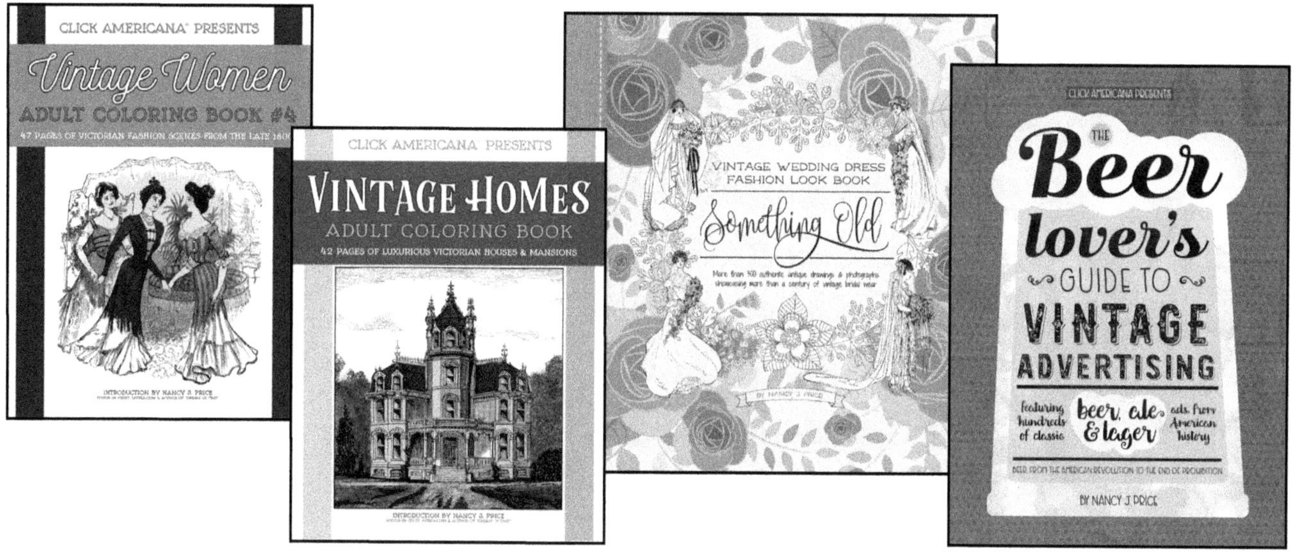

CHECK OUT OUR WEBSITES, TOO...

ClickAmericana.com
Thousands of articles, photos and vintage ads
from throughout American history.

PrintColorFun.com
Hundreds of free coloring pages
to download and print at home.

Myria.com
Smart stuff for real life:
Health, parenting, psychology,
science, tech, entertainment — plus
recipes, home decor & other good things.

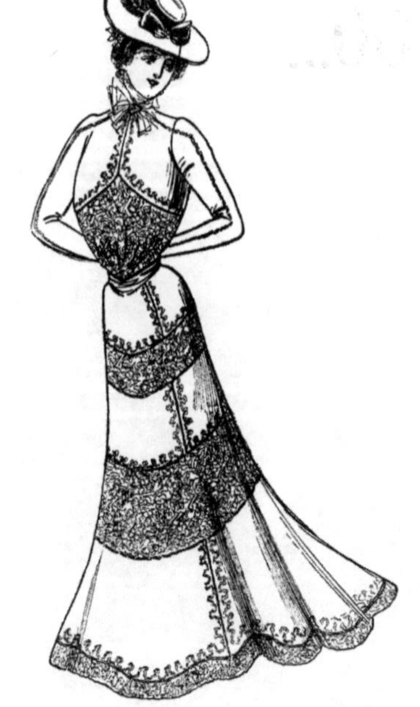

www.ingramcontent.com/pod-product-compliance
Lightning Source LLC
LaVergne TN
LVHW081614110826
845155LV00039BA/192
* 9 7 8 1 9 4 4 6 3 3 3 6 3 *